HMH | (into) Math™

Practice and Homework Journal

Grade 5

ISBN 978-0-358-11156-6

11 12 2677 28 27 26 25 24 23 22

4500857014   C D E F G

Whole Numbers, Expressions, and Volume

Unit 2

Add and Subtract Fractions and Mixed Numbers

Module 6 Understand Addition and Subtraction of Fractions with Unlike Denominators

Module 7 Add and Subtract Fractions and Mixed Numbers with Unlike Denominators

Unit 3 Multiply Fractions and Mixed Numbers

Unit 4 Divide Fractions and Convert Customary Units

© Houghton Mifflin Harcourt Publishing Company

Module 12 Customary Measurement

© Houghton Mifflin Harcourt Publishing Company

Unit 6 Multiply Decimals

Unit 7 — Divide Decimals and Convert Metric Units

Unit 8 Graphs, Patterns, and Geometry

© Houghton Mifflin Harcourt Publishing Company

LESSON 1.1
**More Practice/
Homework**

 ONLINE
Video Tutorials and
Interactive Examples

Recognize the 10 to 1 Relationship Among Place-Value Positions

1 (MP) **Use Tools** How do you know that 30 is $\frac{1}{10}$ of 300? Show your work.

_____

_____

2 What number is $\frac{1}{10}$ of 8,000,000? _____

3 What number is 10 times as much as 50? _____

4 What number is 10 times as much as 3,000? _____

5 What number is $\frac{1}{10}$ of 30,000? _____

6 **Math on the Spot** Mark and Robyn used base-ten blocks to show that 200 is 100 times as much as 2. Whose visual model makes sense? Whose visual model is nonsense? Explain your reasoning.

Mark's Work   **Robyn's Work**

_____200_____   _____   _____200_____   _____

_____   _____

_____   _____

_____   _____

Test Prep

7 How does the place value of the leftmost 3 in 330 compare to the place value of the digit 3 to its right?

_____

_____

8 Select all numbers in which the place value of the digit 6 is equal to $\frac{1}{10}$ of the place value of the digit 6 in the number 760,000.

Ⓐ 3,600

Ⓑ 6,000

Ⓒ 20,600

Ⓓ 256,000

Ⓔ 600,000

Ⓕ 2,765,400

9 What number is 10 times as much as 300,000?

_____

10 What number is $\frac{1}{10}$ of 4,000? _____

Spiral Review

11 Marco is building a fence around a square garden. Each side of the garden is 8 feet long. What is the area of the garden?

_____

12 Portia has 72 postcards. This is 8 times as many as Jonathan has. How many postcards does Jonathan have?

_____

13 Arrange the following numbers in order from least to greatest.

96,432; 94,632; 96,342

_____

14 How many pairs of parallel sides does the hexagon appear to have?

_____

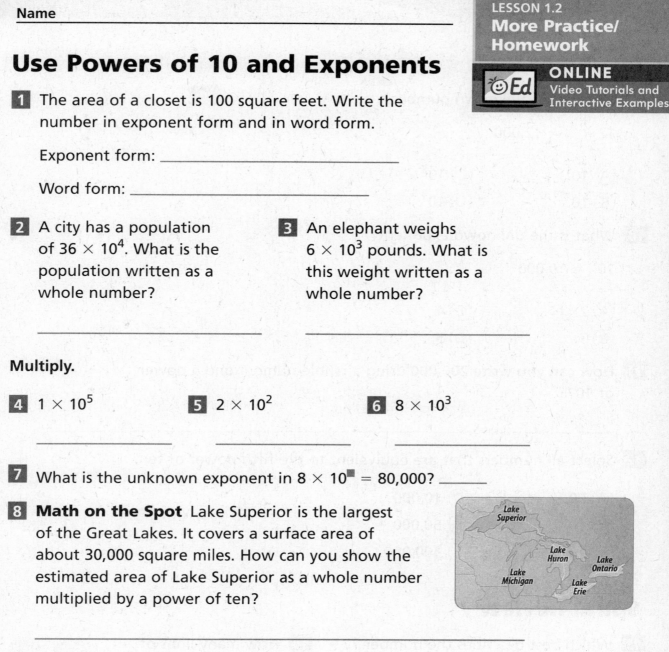

Use Powers of 10 and Exponents

1 The area of a closet is 100 square feet. Write the number in exponent form and in word form.

Exponent form: _____

Word form: _____

2 A city has a population of 36×10^4. What is the population written as a whole number?

3 An elephant weighs 6×10^3 pounds. What is this weight written as a whole number?

_____

Multiply.

4 1×10^5

5 2×10^2

6 8×10^3

_____

7 What is the unknown exponent in $8 \times 10^{\blacksquare} = 80{,}000$? _____

8 **Math on the Spot** Lake Superior is the largest of the Great Lakes. It covers a surface area of about 30,000 square miles. How can you show the estimated area of Lake Superior as a whole number multiplied by a power of ten?

_____

_____

The estimated area of Lake Superior

is _____.

Test Prep

9 What is the unknown number?

$12 \times \blacksquare = 12{,}000$

- (A) 10^1
- (B) 10^2
- (C) 10^3
- (D) 10^4

10 What is the unknown exponent?

$10^{\blacksquare} = 10{,}000$

- (A) 2
- (B) 3
- (C) 4
- (D) 5

11 How can you write 200,000 using a whole number and a power of 10?

_____

12 Select all numbers that are equivalent to the fifth power of ten.

- (A) 50
- (B) 10^4
- (C) 10^5
- (D) 10,000
- (E) 50,000
- (F) 100,000

Spiral Review

13 Which best describes the number 7? Write *prime* or *composite*.

_____

14 How many lines of symmetry does the figure appear to have?

_____

15 Jada has 12 photos. Anthony has 6 times as many photos. How many photos does Anthony have?

_____

16 Juli buys a flat with 48 flowers. She wants to plant them in equal rows of 5 flowers. How many rows can Juli plant? How many flowers will be left over?

_____

LESSON 1.3
**More Practice/
Homework**

Ed **ONLINE**
Video Tutorials and
Interactive Examples

Use a Pattern to Multiply
by Multiples of 10, 100, and 1,000

1 The distance from Seattle to Orlando is about 3,000 miles.
The distance from Earth to the moon is 80 times that distance.
What is the distance from Earth to the moon?

_____

Complete the multiplication fact and pattern.

2 $7 \times 8 =$ _____

$(7 \times 8) \times 10^1 =$ _____

$(7 \times 8) \times 10^2 =$ _____

$(7 \times 8) \times 10^3 =$ _____

3 $8 \times 5 =$ _____

$(8 \times 5) \times 10^1 =$ _____

$(8 \times 5) \times 10^2 =$ _____

$(8 \times 5) \times 10^3 =$ _____

Multiply.

4 $20 \times 800 =$ _____

5 $40 \times 500 =$ _____

6 _____ $= 70 \times 9,000$

7 _____ $= 90 \times 3,000$

8 (MP) **Reason** How many zeros are in the product of any nonzero
whole number less than 10 and 500? Explain your answer.

_____

_____

_____

_____

_____

9 **Math on the Spot** An average person has 6×10^2 times as
many red blood cells as white blood cells. A small sample of
blood has 7×10^3 white blood cells. About how many red blood
cells are in the sample?

_____

Test Prep

10 What is the unknown exponent?

$$50 \times 8,000 = 4 \times 10^{\blacksquare}$$

(A) 3   (C) 5

(B) 4   (D) 6

11 What is the unknown number?

$$30 \times \blacksquare = 150,000$$

(A) 50   (C) 5,000

(B) 500   (D) 50,000

12 What is the product $7,000 \times 50$ written as the product of a whole number and a power of 10?

_____

13 How many zeros are in the product $50 \times 6,000$?

_____

Spiral Review

14 Gina buys 4 packs of stickers for her scrapbook. There are 9 stickers in each pack. Each page in the scrapbook holds 6 stickers. How many pages does Gina need for these stickers?

_____

15 What is the value of the underlined digit?

75,397,809

_____

16 There are 24 students in a math class. The teacher arranges the students into equal groups of 4 students. Each group solves 3 different math problems. How many math problems does the class solve?

_____

17 Marlin was playing basketball and made $\frac{8}{10}$ of the shots he took. What decimal number represents the fraction of shots Marlin made?

_____

Multiply by 1-Digit Numbers

1 There are 7 teachers going to a 5-day math conference. If registration is $225 for each teacher, how much do the teachers pay?

_____

2 A trip to Lauren's grandfather's house is 3,074 miles round trip. If the family visits him 4 times each year, how many miles do they travel to see him in one year?

_____

3 **STEM** A solar panel produces 265 watts of power each day. If 9 solar panels are installed on a house, how much power is produced in one day?

_____

Estimate. Then find the product.

4 Estimate: _____

$$\begin{array}{r} 827 \\ \times\ \ \ 4 \\ \hline \end{array}$$

5 Estimate: _____

$$\begin{array}{r} 3,904 \\ \times\ \ \ \ \ 6 \\ \hline \end{array}$$

6 Estimate: _____

$$\begin{array}{r} 35,923 \\ \times\ \ \ \ \ \ \ 5 \\ \hline \end{array}$$

7 Estimate: _____

$$\begin{array}{r} 629 \\ \times\ \ \ 3 \\ \hline \end{array}$$

8 Estimate: _____

$$\begin{array}{r} 5,038 \\ \times\ \ \ \ \ 7 \\ \hline \end{array}$$

9 Estimate: _____

$$\begin{array}{r} 47,185 \\ \times\ \ \ \ \ \ \ 8 \\ \hline \end{array}$$

Test Prep

10 Select all products that are 2,952.

(A) 8×369

(B) $2 \times 1,426$

(C) 3×984

(D) 6×442

(E) 9×328

11 Each cargo container weighs 2,205 pounds. How much do 9 containers weigh?

(A) 19,805 pounds   (C) 20,205 pounds

(B) 19,845 pounds   (D) 181,845 pounds

12 Raphael worked 7 days in one week and earned $142 per day. How much did Raphael earn that week?

_____

Spiral Review

13 Which symbol makes the statement true? Write $<$, $>$, or $=$.

692,886 ◯ 698,286

14 If each student in the class drinks $1\frac{3}{5}$ cups of juice during the party and there are 9 students in the class, how many cups of juice will be needed?

_____

15 Micah buys 3 packages with 12 stickers in each package. She divides the stickers equally among herself and 5 friends. How many stickers does each person get?

_____

16 A concert is attended by 26,493 people. To the nearest thousand, about how many people attended the concert?

_____

Multiply by Multi-Digit Numbers

1 The map shows the driving distance from Tampa to New York City. The circumference of Earth is 22 times that distance. What is the circumference of Earth?

_____

2 A food service provides 8,952 hot dogs at every baseball game. How many hot dogs does the food service provide for the 81 games during the season?

_____

1,132 miles

Estimate. Then find the product.

3 Estimate: _____

```
   983
×   41
```

4 Estimate: _____

```
 7,185
×   28
```

5 Estimate: _____

```
 3,194
×   57
```

6 Estimate: _____

```
28,736
×   52
```

7 Estimate: _____

```
81,547
×   21
```

8 Estimate: _____

```
   534
× 417
```

9 (MP) **Reason** Find the values for *a*, *b*, and *c* in the multiplication problem.

```
  2 2 3
  1 1 2
   1, 6 a 9
×      4 3
   4, b 7 7
+ 6 6, 3 c 0
   7 1, 3 3 7
```

Test Prep

10 What is 4,337 × 64?

_____

11 The diameter of the Agrippa crater, located on the moon, is 46 kilometers. Earth's diameter is 277 times as long as the diameter of the crater. What is Earth's diameter?

(A) 1,662 km   (C) 12,742 km

(B) 10,102 km   (D) 950,722 km

12 The world's population increases by about 143 people each minute. By how many people does the world's population increase in 6 hours?

_____

13 Select all the products that have a value of 5,544.

(A) 36 × 154

(B) 11 × 540

(C) 28 × 198

(D) 24 × 231

(E) 44 × 124

Spiral Review

14 A car costs $15,927 to build. Which digit is in the thousands place?

_____

15 What is the fifth power of ten written as a whole number?

_____

16 Alfred delivers 10^2 newspapers every week. How many newspapers does Alfred deliver in 14 weeks?

_____

17 The first term in a pattern is 74. The rule is *subtract 10*. What is the sixth term in the pattern?

_____

LESSON 1.6
**More Practice/
Homework**

ONLINE
Video Tutorials and
Interactive Examples

Develop Multiplication Fluency

1 The floorplan shows an L-shaped room. Shane wants to buy carpet for the room. The cost for one square foot of carpet is $4. What is the cost to carpet the room?

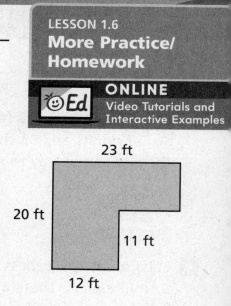

23 ft

20 ft

11 ft

12 ft

_____

2 Mr. Simmons drives 32 miles each day to work and back. Ms. Lee drives 45 miles each day to work and back. Mr. Simmons drove to work and back 232 days last year. Ms. Lee drove to work and back 198 days last year. Who drove more and by how many miles?

_____

3 A building has 18 stories. Each story has a floor that measures 54 feet by 48 feet. What is the area of the floors in the building?

_____

4 Jake buys 12 bags with 144 beads each, Amina buys 16 bags with 85 beads each, and Toni buys 12 bags with 75 beads each. How many beads do they have?

_____

5 Last year, Ms. Giancarlo flew for business 13 times. Each time was 488 miles. Mr. Garcia flew twice for business, once for 1,495 miles and the other for 4,825 miles. Who traveled more miles for business? How many more?

_____

6 A company has 14 offices that need new carpeting. Each office measures 22 feet by 17 feet. How much carpeting does the company need?

_____

7 Last month, an office supply store sold 125 chairs for $68 each and 28 desks for $256 each. What is the total amount of the sales?

_____

Test Prep

8 Train tickets cost $48 for adults and $32 for children. There are 27 adults and 55 children on the train. How much did the passengers pay to ride the train?

(A) $1,296

(C) $3,056

(B) $1,760

(D) $6,560

9 Each square of a chess board measures 57 millimeters by 57 millimeters. There are 64 squares on a chess board. What is the area of the chess board?

_____

10 A toolbox contains 12 screwdrivers and 11 wrenches. Each screwdriver has a mass of 1,298 grams, and each wrench has a mass of 2,282 grams. What is the mass of the screwdrivers and wrenches?

_____

11 The price for 1 ounce of gold is $1,275. How much is 5 pounds of gold worth? Recall that 1 pound = 16 ounces.

_____

Spiral Review

12 What is the word form of 21,572?

_____

_____

13 The rule for a pattern is *add* 7. The first term in the pattern is 8. Write the first six terms of the pattern.

_____

14 Anna ordered 200 party favors. She received only $\frac{1}{10}$ of the party favors she ordered. How many party favors did Anna receive?

_____

15 A farmer packages 144 eggs in each box. How many eggs are there in 7 boxes?

_____

LESSON 2.1
**More Practice/
Homework**

 **ONLINE**
Video Tutorials and
Interactive Examples

Relate Multiplication to Division

1 (MP) **Model with Mathematics** Martin places 51 toy cars in 3 equal rows. How many toy cars are in each row?

- Draw to represent the situation.

- Write a multiplication equation and a division equation to model the situation.

  _____

- How many toy cars are in each row?

  _____

(MP) **Use Structure** Use multiplication and the Distributive Property to find the quotient. Show your work.

2 There are 1,020 entries in a photo contest. Six judges will review an equal number of photos. How many photos will each judge review?

_____

3 Jin schedules 496 hours for a project. He plans to work 8 hours each day. How many days will it take to complete the project?

_____

4 **Math on the Spot** Mr. Henderson has 2 bouncy-ball vending machines. He buys one bag of the 27-millimeter balls and one bag of the 40-millimeter balls. He puts an equal number of each in the 2 machines. How many bouncy balls does he put in each machine?

Bouncy Balls	
Size	Number in Bag
27 mm	180
40 mm	80
mm = millimeters	

_____

Test Prep

5 Select all the expressions that can be used to find the quotient $104 \div 8$.

Ⓐ $(8 \times 10) + (8 \times 3)$

Ⓑ $(8 + 10) \times (8 + 3)$

Ⓒ $8 \times (4 + 9)$

Ⓓ $(8 \times 5) + (8 \times 8)$

Ⓔ $8 + (5 \times 8)$

6 Write a related multiplication equation that could be used to solve the following division problem.

$216 \div 6 = \blacksquare$

_____

7 The floor area of a rectangular room is 162 square feet. The width of the room is 9 feet. What is the length?

_____

Spiral Review

8 How is the value of the digit 5 in 465,200 related to the value of the digit 5 in 652,400?

_____

_____

9 A clothing store orders 15 boxes of shirts to restock their shelves. There are 125 shirts in each box. How many shirts does the clothing store order?

_____

10 What number is $\frac{1}{10}$ of 8,000?

11 What is the product 7×10^6?

_____

Represent Division with 2-Digit Divisors

1 (MP) **Model with Mathematics** The Nile River is the longest river in the world, measuring 6,650 kilometers long. The Nile River is 50 times longer than Japan's Omono River. How long is the Omono River?

- Draw a visual model to represent the situation.

- Write a division equation to model and solve this situation.

_____

(MP) **Use Tools** Use an area model to represent the division equation and find the quotient.

2 $3,860 \div 20 = g$

3 $c = 732 \div 12$

4 (MP) **Model with Mathematics** Write a division equation that relates to the following application of the Distributive Property.

$$18 \times (200 + 9) = (18 \times 200) + (18 \times 9)$$

$$= 3,600 + 162$$

$$= 3,762$$

_____

5 **Math on the Spot** Two Pony Express riders each rode part of a 216-mile trip. Each rider rode the same number of miles. They changed horses every 12 miles. How many horses did each

rider use? _____

Test Prep

6 Luisa needs to complete the area model to find 946 ÷ 22. Which equation represents the solution shown in the area model?

	■	■	■
22	22 × 20 = 440	22 × 20 = 440	22 × 3 = 66

(A) 20 + 20 + 3 = 43

(B) 22 + 20 + 3 = 45

(C) 22 + 22 + 3 = 47

(D) 22 + 22 + 22 = 66

7 A bill for $1,896 is paid in 12 monthly installments. The same amount must be paid each month. Each installment will be divided equally between two people. How much

does each person pay each month? _____

8 There are 128 fluid ounces in a gallon and 16 fluid ounces in a pint. Shelby wants to find the number of pints in a gallon. She writes a multiplication equation and a division equation to represent this situation. Place the numbers into the correct boxes.

16   8   128

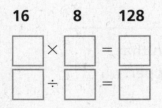

How many pints are in one gallon? _____

Spiral Review

9 Estimate 7 × 896. Then find the product.

Estimate: _____

7 × 896 = _____

10 Estimate 12 × 328. Then find the product.

Estimate: _____

12 × 328 = _____

Estimate with 2-Digit Divisors

1 William buys a gallon of milk from the store. He wants to pour the milk equally into 12 glasses. What is a reasonable estimate for the number of fluid ounces poured into each glass?

1 gallon = 128 fluid ounces

_____

2 (MP) **Construct Arguments** A $94 restaurant bill is divided equally among 15 friends. Is $5 a reasonable estimate of the amount each friend will pay for the bill? Explain.

_____

_____

_____

3 Consumers spend about 1,820 hours per year on their mobile devices. There are 52 weeks in a year. What is a reasonable estimate for the number of hours consumers spend on mobile devices each week?

_____

4 A shipment of 33 containers weighs a total of 6,580 pounds. If each container weighs the same amount, what is a reasonable estimate for the weight of each container?

_____

Use compatible numbers to find two estimates.

5 5,684 ÷ 90

6 628 ÷ 15

_____

7 **Open Ended** Division of a number by a two-digit number results in a reasonable estimate of 100. Write a division equation that would result in such an estimate.

_____

Test Prep

8 A gross is equal to 144 items. A baker's dozen is equal to 13 items. What is a reasonable estimate for the number of baker's dozens in a gross? Show how you found your estimate.

_____

9 Courtney earns $2,574 for 32 days of work. She earns the same amount each day. About how much does she earn each day? What are two reasonable estimates the answer is between?

_____

10 Banil needs to divide 8,951 ÷ 94. He estimates and says that the answer is a 3-digit number. Is that a reasonable claim? Explain.

_____

_____

_____

_____

Spiral Review

11 A coach forms 5 teams for 80 volleyball players. Use multiplication and the Distributive Property to find the number of players on each team.

_____

12 Aniyah arranges 378 seashells into 18 equal rows for a science display. How many seashells are in each row?

_____

Use Partial Quotients

1 **Health and Fitness** Physical activity is important for good health and can reduce the risk of many diseases. During 31 days last summer, a cyclist rode the same number of miles every day for a total of 1,085 miles. How many miles did she ride each day?

_____

2 A hobby shop sells specialty kites for $14 each during a sale. The hobby shop earns $994 on the kite sales. How many kites does the hobby shop sell?

_____

3 An outdoors company donates 1,036 swim vests to be shared equally among 74 swimming programs. How many swim vests does each program receive?

_____

Divide.

4 $723 \div 44$ **5** $4,917 \div 33$ **6** $8,632 \div 29$

_____   _____   _____

7 (MP) **Use Repeated Reasoning** Carmen and Eduardo divide 9,253 by 47 using partial quotients. They both use a multiple of 47 to divide. Carmen uses the multiple 470. Eduardo uses the multiple 940. Whose solution process will require fewer steps? Explain.

_____

_____

8 **Math on the Spot** In a study, 9 people ate a total of 1,566 pounds of potatoes in 2 years. If each person ate the same amount each year, how many pounds of potatoes did each person eat in 1 year?

_____

Test Prep

9 A banquet hall can seat 14 people to a table. An event will have 581 adults and 208 children in attendance. How many tables will have to be set up to seat everyone?

Ⓐ 41

Ⓑ 42

Ⓒ 56

Ⓓ 57

10 There are 448 grams of carbohydrates in a box of cereal. The box contains 16 servings. How many grams of carbohydrates are in one serving?

_____

11 Joby divides 6,792 by 54 using partial quotients. He chooses to use the multiple 1,620 to divide. Select all statements that apply.

Ⓐ Joby multiplies 54 by 30 to get 1,620, so his partial quotient is 30.

Ⓑ Joby subtracts 1,620 from 6,792 to see how much of the dividend is left.

Ⓒ Joby divides 6,792 by about 4 to get 1,620, so his partial quotient is 4.

Ⓓ Joby adds 1,620 to 540 to get his next partial quotient.

Ⓔ Joby divides 1,620 by 4 to get the final answer.

Spiral Review

12 Raul takes 235 pictures on his summer vacation. If he puts 5 pictures on each page of his scrapbook, how many pages will his scrapbook have?

13 All 256 fifth-grade students are going to see the new play downtown. If there are 8 buses each taking an equal number of students to see the play, how many students are on each bus?

© Houghton Mifflin Harcourt Publishing Company

Name _____

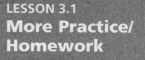

ONLINE Video Tutorials and Interactive Examples

Divide by 2-Digit Divisors

1 Marsha is arranging the seats for an award ceremony. She has 322 chairs that she has to arrange into 14 equal rows. How many chairs will Marsha have in each row?

_____

2 **Math on the Spot** The Smoothie shop has 1,360 ounces of cranberry juice and 710 ounces of passion fruit juice. If the juices are used to make Crazy Cranberry smoothies, which juice will run out first? How much of the other juice will be left over?

Smoothie Main Ingredients		
Orange Tango	18 oz orange juice	12 oz mango juice
Crazy Cranberry	20 oz cranberry juice	10 oz passion fruit juice
Royal Purple	22 oz grape juice	8 oz apple juice

_____

_____

3 **(MP) Reason** The new theater has 465 seats arranged into sections. If there are 17 sections in the theater, how many seats could be in each section?

_____

Divide. Show your work.

4 1,150 ÷ 25

5 805 ÷ 35

6 2,594 ÷ 52

7 927 ÷ 13

© Houghton Mifflin Harcourt Publishing Company

Test Prep

8 There are 208 science fair projects that will be spread out equally over 16 tables. How many projects will be displayed on each table?

(A) 10   (B) 12   (C) 13   (D) 16

9 A store has a collection of 156 dolls. The store has 13 shelves and wants to place the same number of dolls on each shelf. How many dolls should be placed on each shelf?

(A) 10   (B) 11   (C) 12   (D) 13

10 A company has 2,364 tickets for a county fair. If the tickets are shared equally among 14 schools, how many tickets will each school receive?

(A) 169

(B) 168

(C) 159

(D) 158

Spiral Review

11 Complete the multiplication fact and pattern.

$6 \times 5 =$ _____ $6 \times 500 =$ _____

$6 \times 50 =$ _____ $6 \times 5,000 =$ _____

12 Draw an area model to represent the division equation and find the quotient.

$4,360 \div 20 =$ _____

LESSON 3.2
**More Practice/
Homework**

ONLINE
Video Tutorials and
Interactive Examples

Interpret the Remainder

1 **Geography** The average depth of the ocean is about 3,688 meters. You would have to stack the tallest tower of the Incheon Bridge in South Korea 16 times to reach this depth. What is the height, in meters, of the tallest tower on the Incheon Bridge?

_____

2 (MP) **Reason** A group of students is taking a field trip. Each bus holds 24 students. If 174 students are going on the trip, how many buses will be needed to hold everyone?

_____

_____

3 **Open Ended** Write a word problem that can be modeled by the expression 193 ÷ 14.

_____

_____

_____

_____

4 **Math on the Spot** James has 884 feet of rope. There are 12 teams of hikers. If James gives an equal amount of rope to each team, how much rope will each team receive?

_____

Divide. Interpret the remainder to solve.

5 The owner of a snack bar wants to put 294 ounces of trail mix into bags. If 16 ounces are put into each bag, how many bags can be completely filled?

_____

6 A restaurant has a supply of 796 forks. Twelve forks are needed to completely set one table. How many tables can be completely set?

_____

Test Prep

7 Chris needs to cut a roll of twine into 16 equal lengths for a project. If the roll of twine measures 900 inches, how long will each length of twine measure?

_____

8 There are 382 participants in a boat-racing competition. Each boat holds 13 people. How many boats are needed so that everyone can participate?

Ⓐ 28
Ⓑ 29
Ⓒ 30
Ⓓ 31

9 Martin orders 285 anoles for his reptile shop. If he divides the anoles equally among 16 tanks, how many are left for the last tank?

Ⓐ 9
Ⓑ 11
Ⓒ 13
Ⓓ 15

10 There are 186 blueberries in a bag. If 12 blueberries are placed in each bowl of fruit salad, how many bowls of fruit salad can be made using one bag of blueberries?

Ⓐ 12   Ⓑ 15   Ⓒ 16   Ⓓ 18

Spiral Review

11 Estimate. Then find the product.

Estimate: _____

$$\begin{array}{r} 836 \\ \times\ \ \ 6 \\ \hline \end{array}$$

12 Use compatible numbers to find an estimate.

2,348 ÷ 40

_____

© Houghton Mifflin Harcourt Publishing Company

Name _____

LESSON 3.3
**More Practice/
Homework**

Ed **ONLINE**
Video Tutorials and
Interactive Examples

Adjust Quotients

1 **(MP)** **Reason** A popular author brings 8,428 copies of her new book on her book tour. She sells 85 books at each book signing. She makes two estimates to determine how many book signings it will take to sell all of her books: $8,400 \div 70 = 120$ and $8,100 \div 90 = 90$.

Use each estimate to divide. What adjustments, if any, must be made using each estimate?

_____

_____

_____

2 A store sells trading cards. The store has 1,173 baseball cards, 692 basketball cards, and 445 football cards and wants to put all of them in albums. Each page in the albums holds 15 cards. How many pages are needed to hold all of the cards?

_____

Write a division equation that estimates the value of the expression. Then use your estimate to divide, adjusting numbers as needed.

3 $3,694 \div 79$ **4** $1,326 \div 29$ **5** $947 \div 46$

_____   _____   _____

Describe the estimated digit in the whole-number quotient as *too high*, *too low*, or *correct*. Adjust the estimated digit if needed. Then divide.

6 $\overset{8}{64)\overline{4,729}}$ **7** $\overset{4}{29)\overline{1,262}}$ **8** $\overset{8}{42)\overline{3,288}}$

_____   _____   _____

Test Prep

9 A shop owner wants to buy a new laptop. The laptop costs $1,485. How many weeks will the owner have to save if he saves $50 each week?

(A) 20 weeks

(B) 29 weeks

(C) 30 weeks

(D) 31 weeks

10 A shipment of 53 new television sets weighs 2,968 pounds. How much does each television weigh?

(A) 50 pounds

(B) 56 pounds

(C) 58 pounds

(D) 60 pounds

11 Describe the estimated digit in the whole-number quotient as *too high*, *too low*, or *correct*. Adjust the estimated digit if needed. Then divide.

$$\overset{4}{32)\overline{1,229}}$$

_____

12 Mrs. Benson pays the same amount each month to ride the train to work. She pays $1,428 for 24 months. Which shows the best estimate for the amount she pays each month?

(A) $1,400 \div 20$

(B) $1,400 \div 30$

(C) $1,500 \div 20$

(D) $1,000 \div 30$

Spiral Review

13 Multiply.

$4,359 \times 45$

14 Divide. Use partial quotients.

$5,726 \div 23$

LESSON 3.4
**More Practice/
Homework**

ONLINE
Video Tutorials and
Interactive Examples

Practice with Division

1 (MP) **Use Tools** The gift shop sold 4 times as much
wrapping paper in December as in January. They sold
635 rolls over the two months.

- Draw a bar model to represent the number sold each month.

- Write an equation to show the number represented by each
box of the bar model. Then find the number.

  _____

- How much wrapping paper was sold in December? Explain
how you know.

  _____

  _____

2 (MP) **Use Structure** The crew on a boat catch four fish that weigh
a total of 240 pounds. The king mackerel weighs twice as much as
the blackfin tuna, and the wahoo weighs twice as much as the
king mackerel. The weight of the sailfish is 5 times as much as the
blackfin tuna. How much does each fish weigh?

  _____

3 (MP) **Use Tools** A new machine makes 3 times as many toys
in one hour as the old machine. If both machines make a total
of 248 toys in one hour, how many toys does the new machine
make in one hour?

- Draw a bar model to represent the situation.

- How many toys does the new machine make in one hour?

  _____

Test Prep

4 A new carpet cleaning company claims that they can clean 3 times as many carpets in one week as another company. If both companies combined can clean 332 carpets in one week, how many carpets does the new company clean?

(A) 249

(B) 252

(C) 316

(D) 362

5 Which division expression could be used to find the value of one box represented in the bar model?

(A) 756 ÷ 9

(B) 756 ÷ 8

(C) 756 ÷ 7

(D) 756 ÷ 6

6 Jenna and Maryse are comparing how many books they read during the last two years. Together, they read 267 books. How many books did Jenna read if she read twice as many as Maryse?

(A) 89

(B) 134

(C) 167

(D) 178

Spiral Review

7 A typical soccer field measures 110 meters long and 73 meters wide. What is the total area of the soccer field?

8 There are 204 seats in the new balcony level at the stadium. If there are 12 rows with an equal number of seats, how many seats are in each row?

Write Numerical Expressions

1 (MP) **Model with Mathematics** One small airplane has 44 seats. The flight crew sits in two of these seats. The remaining seats are divided equally into 7 rows for passengers. Explain how you would write a numerical expression to model the number of seats in each passenger row.

_____

_____

_____

2 **Health and Fitness** Masha is training for a marathon. She is doing tempo runs to increase her speed. In tempo runs, a runner varies their pace during the run. Masha jogs 1 mile, then runs at a fast pace for 11 miles. She finishes by walking 2 miles to cool down. Write a numerical expression to model the number of miles Masha runs, walks, or jogs.

_____

3 Write a numerical expression to model the words. Subtract 1 from the product of 4 and 5.

_____

4 **Math on the Spot** There are tiger barbs in a 30-gallon aquarium and giant danios in a 20-gallon aquarium. Write a numerical expression to represent the greatest total number of fish that could be in both aquariums. Use the rule and the table to solve this problem.

The rule for the number of fish in an aquarium is to allow 1 gallon of water for each inch of length.

Aquarium Fish	
Type of Fish	**Length (in inches)**
Lemon Tetra	2
Strawberry Tetra	3
Giant Danio	5
Tiger Barb	3
Swordtail	5

_____

Test Prep

5 Write a numerical expression to model the words.

Divide 60 by 5.

_____

6 Which of the following can be modeled by the numerical expression $(16 - 4) \div 2$? Select all that apply.

(A) Subtract 4 from 16 and then divide the difference by 2.

(B) Find the difference of 16 and the quotient of 4 and 2.

(C) Divide 16 by the difference of 4 and 2.

(D) Divide the difference of 16 and 4 by 2.

(E) Subtract the quotient of 4 and 2 from 16.

7 Which numerical expression models the following words?

Multiply 2 by the sum of 8 and 4.

(A) $8 \times 2 + 4$

(B) $8 + (4 \times 2)$

(C) $(8 + 4) \times 2$

(D) $8 + (2 \times 4)$

8 Write a numerical expression to model the words.

Divide 10 by the difference of 5 and 3.

_____

Spiral Review

9 Divide.

$165 \div 11 =$ _____

$154 \div 14 =$ _____

10 Divide.

$306 \div 17 =$ _____

$322 \div 14 =$ _____

© Houghton Mifflin Harcourt Publishing Company

LESSON 4.2
**More Practice/
Homework**

ONLINE
Video Tutorials and
Interactive Examples

Interpret Numerical Expressions

1 (MP) **Critique Reasoning** Rafiq compares the expressions 4×8 and 8×12. He says that 8 is twice as much as 4, so 4×8 must be twice as much as 8×12. Correct his statement, and explain his error.

_____

_____

_____

_____

Compare the numerical expressions.

2 $24 + 7$ and $9 \times (24 + 7)$

_____

_____

3 $12 - 7$ and $4 \times (12 - 7)$

_____

_____

4 $3 \times (21 + 4)$ and $21 + 4$

_____

_____

5 40×5 and 40×20

_____

_____

6 (MP) **Reason** Tina says that she can compare the expressions 3×10 and 15×20 without multiplying them. Explain how she could compare the factors to compare the expressions without multiplying them.

_____

_____

_____

_____

Test Prep

7 Compare the numerical expressions.

$$24 \times 12 \text{ and } 4 \times 12$$

_____

8 Which of these statements best describes the relationship between $7 \times (18 - 5)$ and $18 - 5$?

- (A) $7 \times (18 - 5)$ is 7 times as great as $18 - 5$.
- (B) $18 - 5$ is 7 times as great as $7 \times (18 - 5)$.
- (C) $7 \times (18 - 5)$ is 18 times as great as $18 - 5$.
- (D) $18 - 5$ is 18 times as great as $7 \times (18 - 5)$.

9 Select all expressions that are twice as great as 12×7.

- (A) 12×27
- (B) 24×7
- (C) 2×7
- (D) 12×14
- (E) 24×14

10 Compare the numerical expressions.

$$9 - 4 \text{ and } 4 \times (9 - 4)$$

_____

Spiral Review

11 Josie works a total of 85 hours a month. If she works for the next 9 months, how many hours does Josie work?

12 Use multiplication and the Distributive Property to find $175 \div 5$. Show your work.

_____

LESSON 4.3
**More Practice/
Homework**

 ONLINE
Video Tutorials and
Interactive Examples

Evaluate Numerical Expressions

1 (MP) **Critique Reasoning** Anthony writes the
numerical expression 2 + 10 × 3 − 2 and says the
expression has a value of 34. Is Anthony correct?
Explain your answer.

_____

_____

_____

_____

Evaluate the numerical expression.

2 5 × (7 + 4) − 8

3 3 × 8 − 6 × 3

4 120 − 20 ÷ 10 + 2

5 5 + 3 × 4 + 1

6 **STEM** An Arctic
tern has the longest
migration pattern of
any animal. It migrates
about five times the
combined distance that

Distances Migrated in a Year	
Pacific loggerhead turtle	12,000 kilometers
Hummingbird	2,000 kilometers

a Pacific loggerhead turtle and hummingbird migrate. Write a
numerical expression to model the distance that an Arctic tern
migrates. About how far does an Arctic tern migrate?

_____

7 **Math on the Spot** Write and evaluate two equivalent
numerical expressions that show the Distributive Property
of Multiplication.

_____

Test Prep

8 Evaluate the numerical expression $3 + 8 \times (7 - 4)$.

_____

9 A numerical expression is evaluated as shown.

$$2 \times 5 + (4 \times 7) - 5$$

Step 1: $2 \times 5 + 28 - 5$

Step 2: $2 \times 33 - 5$

Step 3: $66 - 5$

Step 4: 61

In which step does an error first appear?

(A) Step 1   (C) Step 3

(B) Step 2   (D) Step 4

10 Select all the expressions in which subtraction is the first operation you perform when evaluating it.

(A) $3 \times 6 + 14 - 9$

(B) $12 \times (15 - 9)$

(C) $18 \div (6 \div 3) - 4$

(D) $9 - 3 + 14 - 6$

(E) $(10 - 4) \div 2$

11 Write and evaluate a numerical expression for the sum of the three addends 8, 10, and 6 divided by 3.

_____

Spiral Review

12 Each box can hold 12 cans. If there are 140 cans, how many boxes are needed?

13 Divide.

$2,028 \div 26$

_____

Use Grouping Symbols

1 ⓜ **Model with Mathematics** Dan has a flower shop. He has a display of 36 roses. He sells 3 bouquets of 4 roses on Monday and 2 bouquets of 5 roses on Tuesday. What expression models the number of roses Dan has left in the display?

_____

2 ⓜ **Reason** Describe how you would evaluate the numerical expression.

$$\{[24 \div (6 - 2)] - 4\} \times 3$$

_____

_____

_____

Use parentheses to rewrite the numerical expression to have the given value.

3 $36 \div 9 + 3 - 2$

value: 1

_____

4 $20 - 2 \times 4 + 1$

value: 10

_____

5 $15 + 17 \div 8 - 4$

value: 8

_____

6 $12 - 3 \times 8 - 6$

value: 66

_____

7 ⓜ **Critique Reasoning** Anthony says that he can evaluate the numerical expression $(5 + 4) \times 3 - 2$ without parentheses and get the same answer. Is Anthony correct? Explain how you know.

_____

_____

_____

_____

Test Prep

8 Use parentheses to rewrite the numerical expression
$25 - 4 \times 3 + 2$ to have a value of 11.

_____

9 Select all numerical expressions that have a value of 28.

Ⓐ $3 \times 4 + 2 \times 5 + 6$

Ⓑ $3 \times (4 + 2 \times 5 + 6)$

Ⓒ $3 \times (4 + 2) \times 5 + 6$

Ⓓ $(3 \times 4) + (2 \times 5) + 6$

Ⓔ $(3 \times 4 + 2) \times 5 + 6$

10 Use the numbers 1 through 5 to place the steps in order to
correctly evaluate the numerical expression.

$5 + 60 \div \{6 \times [6 - (1 + 4)]\}$

Step Number	Step
	Multiply the value in the brackets by 6.
	Add 1 and 4.
	Divide 60 by the value in the braces.
	Add 5 to the quotient.
	Subtract the value in the parentheses from 6.

Spiral Review

11 The printer in the library prints
78 pages in one minute. How long
does it take to print 1,950 pages?

12 Write a numerical expression to
model the situation.

Kristen read her book for 2 hours
after school. Then she read for
another hour before she went
to sleep.

_____

Name _____

LESSON 5.1
**More Practice/
Homework**

⊙Ed **ONLINE**
Video Tutorials and
Interactive Examples

Use Unit Cubes to Build Solid Figures

1 **Open Ended** Describe two different right rectangular prisms that can be made using 24 unit cubes.

_____

2 **(MP) Reason** Jun builds a right rectangular prism using ten layers of the unit cubes shown. How many unit cubes are in the right rectangular prism? Explain how you know.

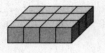

_____

_____

Count the number of cubes used to build each solid figure.

3

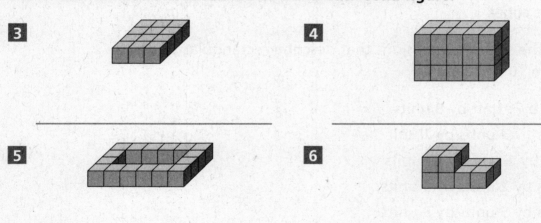

4

_____

5

6

_____   _____

7 **STEM** The Rotterdam cube houses, in the Netherlands, were built in the 1970s. Each house is a cube tilted on one vertex and standing on a pillar. Ravi is making a model of one of these houses using sugar cubes. If one edge of the cube in his model is 5 sugar cubes long, how many sugar cubes will he use? Explain.

_____

_____

Test Prep

8 How many unit cubes are used to make the figure?

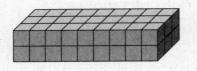

_____

9 Which of the following gives the number of unit cubes used to make this figure?

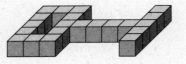

(A) 20 unit cubes

(B) 21 unit cubes

(C) 34 unit cubes

(D) 40 unit cubes

10 Select all the sets of dimensions that describe rectangular prisms made from 10 unit cubes.

(A) 1 unit by 1 unit by 8 units

(B) 2 units by 5 units by 1 unit

(C) 1 unit by 1 unit by 10 units

(D) 2 units by 2 units by 5 units

(E) 2 units by 5 units by 5 units

Spiral Review

11 Write a numerical expression to match the words.

Brian has 24 cookies that he shares equally among 3 friends.

_____

12 Evaluate the numerical expression.

$9 \times 7 + (3 + 4)$

_____

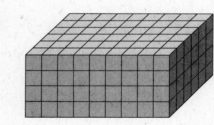
Name _____

Understand Volume

1 (MP) **Attend to Precision** Find the dimensions of the right rectangular prism shown in the diagram. The unit cube represents a volume of 1 cubic inch.

_____

_____

2 (MP) **Use Structure** Ji builds a right rectangular prism with 14 centimeter cubes in the bottom layer with no gaps or overlaps. If there are 8 layers, what is the volume of the right rectangular prism?

_____

Find the volume in cubic units.

3

4

_____   _____

Use the unit given. Find the volume.

5

1 cm 1 cm
1 cm

6

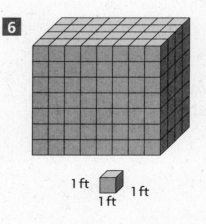

1 ft 1 ft
1 ft

_____   _____

Test Prep

7 The right rectangular prism at the right is made of cubes that are 1 inch on an edge. What is the volume of this figure?

_____

8 Which of the following gives the volume of the figure?

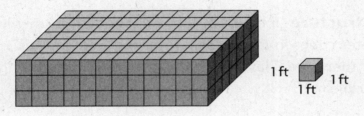

(A) 84 cu ft

(B) 216 cu ft

(C) 231 cu ft

(D) 252 cu ft

1 ft   1 ft
1 ft

9 Select all dimensions that describe right rectangular prisms with a volume greater than 100 cubic units.

(A) 10 units by 4 units by 1 unit

(B) 20 units by 2 units by 3 units

(C) 5 units by 5 units by 5 units

(D) 4 units by 4 units by 7 units

(E) 3 units by 4 units by 8 units

Spiral Review

10 Evaluate the numerical expression.

$7 \times 1 - (3 + 2)$

_____

11 Evaluate the numerical expression.

$4 + (16 - 4) + (12 - 9)$

_____

12 Rewrite the expression with parentheses to equal the given value.

$3 \times 8 - 5 + 3$

value: 12

_____

13 Rewrite the expression with parentheses to equal the given value.

$2 + 5 \times 4 - 2$

value: 12

_____

LESSON 5.3
**More Practice/
Homework**

ONLINE
Video Tutorials and
Interactive Examples

Estimate Volume

1 **Math on the Spot** Marcelle estimated the
volumes of the two boxes using one of his books.
His book has a volume of 48 cubic inches. Box 1
holds about 7 layers of books, and Box 2 holds
about 14 layers of books. Marcelle says that the
volume of either box is about the same. Does
Marcelle's statement make sense or is it nonsense?
Explain your answer.

Box 1   Box 2

_____

_____

_____

Estimate the number of smaller boxes that fit inside the larger box.

2

_____

3

_____

Estimate the volume of the large box.

4 Volume of smaller box: 16 cu in.

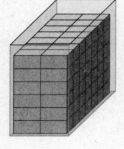

_____

5 Volume of smaller box: 50 cu cm

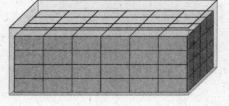

_____

Test Prep

6 The table lists items that are shipped in a large container by an office supply company. Match the description of the container with its estimated volume in cubic centimeters.

	about 24,000 cu cm	about 40,000 cu cm	about 64,000 cu cm	about 72,000 cu cm
40 boxes of paper with a volume of 1,800 cu cm each	☐	☐	☐	☐
500 boxes of staples with a volume of 80 cu cm each	☐	☐	☐	☐
240 boxes of pencils with a volume of 100 cu cm each	☐	☐	☐	☐

7 A book store receives a shipment of books. Each book has a volume of 24 cubic inches. The diagram shows how many books are in the shipment. Estimate the volume of the box filled with books.

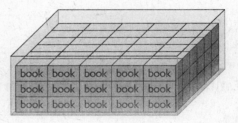

8 The volume of each smaller box is 8 cubic centimeters. Estimate the volume of the larger box.

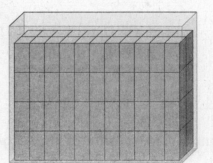

Spiral Review

9 How many unit cubes are used to build the figure?

10 Evaluate the numerical expression.

$(10 - 2) \times (3 + 1)$

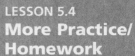

Find Volume of Right Rectangular Prisms

1 One layer of 1-inch cubes is shown. If 9 layers are stacked, what is the volume of the right rectangular prism formed by the stack?

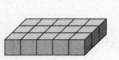

2 **Math on the Spot** Rich is building a travel crate for his dog, Thomas, a beagle-mix who is about 28 inches long, 14 inches wide, and 22 inches tall. For Thomas to travel safely, his crate needs to be a rectangular prism that is about 12 inches greater than his length and width and 6 inches greater than his height. What is the volume of the travel crate that Rich should build?

_____

_____

_____

Find the volume.

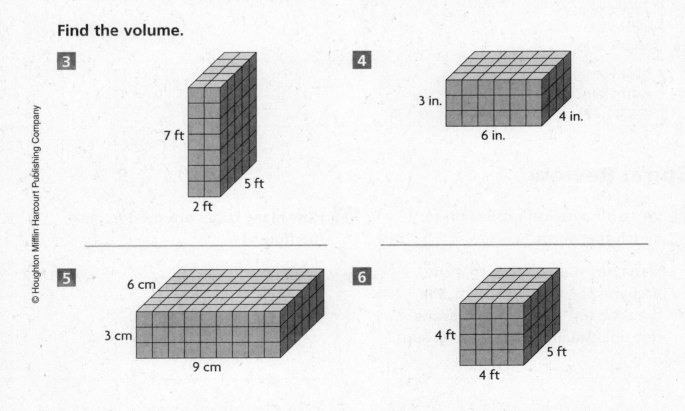

3

7 ft
5 ft
2 ft

4

3 in.
4 in.
6 in.

5

6 cm
3 cm
9 cm

6

4 ft
5 ft
4 ft

Test Prep

7 What is the volume of the right rectangular prism?

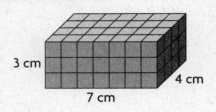

3 cm
7 cm
4 cm

_____

8 Select the volume for each set of dimensions of a right rectangular prism.

	36 cu in.	54 cu in.	72 cu in.
length: 6 in. width: 2 in. height: 3 in.	☐	☐	☐
length: 9 in. width: 3 in. height: 2 in.	☐	☐	☐
length: 4 in. width: 3 in. length: 6 in.	☐	☐	☐
length: 4 in. width: 3 in. length: 3 in.	☐	☐	☐

Spiral Review

9 Write a numerical expression to match the words.

Illana has 16 test tubes that she prepares for the science lab. She breaks 2 test tubes. She gives the rest out equally to the 7 lab groups.

_____

10 How many cubes are used to make the figure?

_____

LESSON 5.5
**More Practice/
Homework**

 ONLINE
Video Tutorials and
Interactive Examples

Apply Volume Formulas

1 (MP) **Use Structure** Nicole designs a jewelry box in the shape of a right rectangular prism. The height is 2 inches. The length is three times as long as the height, and the width is twice as long as the height. If the box needs to have a volume greater than 50 cubic inches, will her design work? Why or why not?

_____

Find the volume.

2

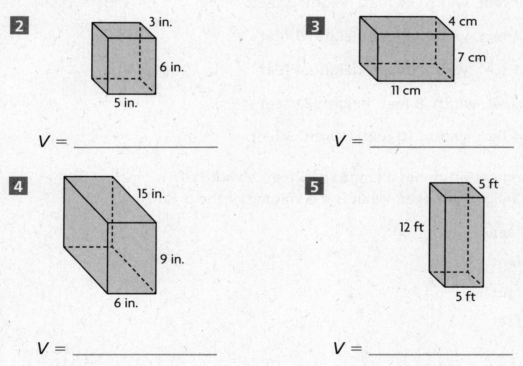

3 in.

6 in.

5 in.

V = _____

3

4 cm

7 cm

11 cm

V = _____

4

15 in.

9 in.

6 in.

V = _____

5

5 ft

12 ft

5 ft

V = _____

6 **History** After skyscrapers first started being built in the United States, the government passed the Height of Buildings Act of 1899. This act made laws for the maximum heights allowed for types of buildings in Washington, D.C. If a wooden building in the shape of a rectangular prism was built to the maximum height of 12 meters, what would be the volume of the building if its base measured 20 meters by 15 meters? Write an equation to show how you found your answer.

_____

Test Prep

7 A package is in the shape of a right rectangular prism with the dimensions shown.

What is the volume of the package?

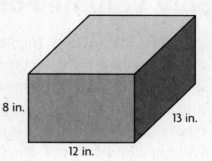

8 in.
12 in.
13 in.

_____

8 Select all the dimensions that a right rectangular prism with a volume of 756 cubic feet can have.

Ⓐ length: 12 feet, width: 14 feet, height: 3 feet

Ⓑ length: 14 feet, width: 6 feet, height: 9 feet

Ⓒ length: 21 feet, width: 9 feet, height: 4 feet

Ⓓ length: 3 feet, width: 8 feet, height: 21 feet

Ⓔ length: 14 feet, width: 18 feet, height: 3 feet

9 A right rectangular prism has a length of 5 feet, a width of 3 feet, and a height of 2 feet. What is the volume of the prism?

Ⓐ 10 cubic feet

Ⓑ 15 cubic feet

Ⓒ 30 cubic feet

Ⓓ 60 cubic feet

Spiral Review

10 How many unit cubes are in the solid figure?

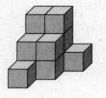

11 Evaluate the expression.

$12 + (19 - 13) \div 6$

_____

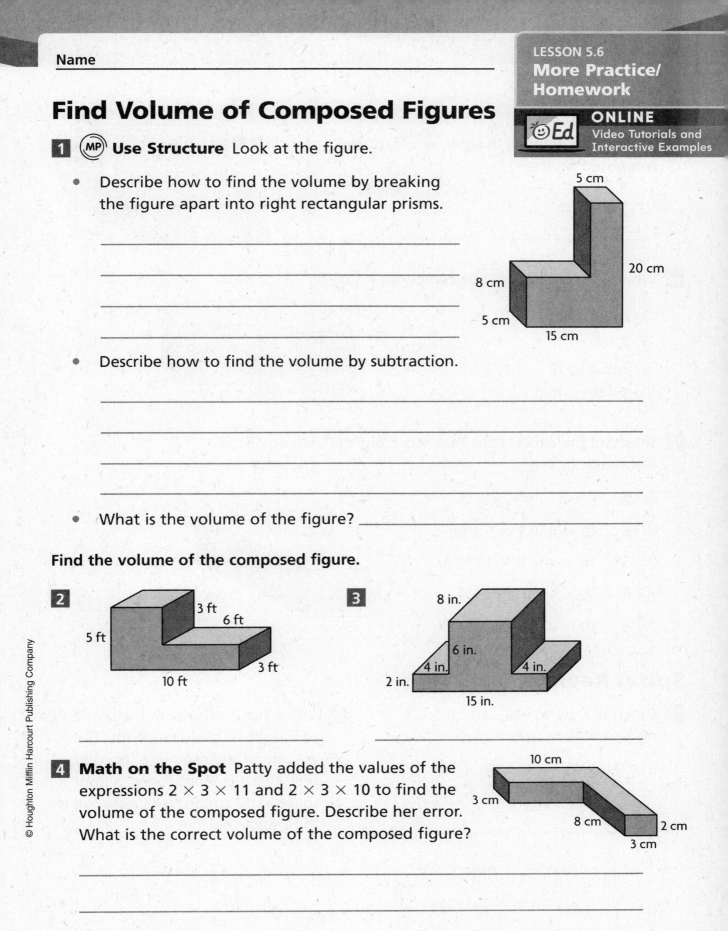

Name _____

Find Volume of Composed Figures

ONLINE
Ed Video Tutorials and
Interactive Examples

1 (MP) **Use Structure** Look at the figure.

- Describe how to find the volume by breaking the figure apart into right rectangular prisms.

_____

_____

_____

_____

- Describe how to find the volume by subtraction.

_____

_____

_____

_____

- What is the volume of the figure? _____

Find the volume of the composed figure.

2

3

_____

4 **Math on the Spot** Patty added the values of the expressions 2 × 3 × 11 and 2 × 3 × 10 to find the volume of the composed figure. Describe her error. What is the correct volume of the composed figure?

_____

_____

_____

© Houghton Mifflin Harcourt Publishing Company

Test Prep

5 What is the volume, in cubic inches, of the composed figure?

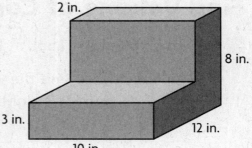

_____

6 What is the volume of the composed figure?

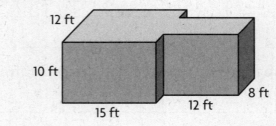

(A) 2,400 cu ft

(B) 2,760 cu ft

(C) 2,952 cu ft

(D) 3,240 cu ft

7 Select all the expressions that represent the volume of the composed figure.

(A) $8 \times 5 \times 4 + 5 \times 5 \times 4$

(B) $5 \times 10 \times 4 + 3 \times 5 \times 4$

(C) $5 \times 10 \times 4 + 8 \times 10 \times 4$

(D) $8 \times 10 \times 4 - 3 \times 5 \times 4$

(E) $8 \times 10 \times 4 - 5 \times 5 \times 4$

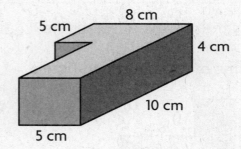

Spiral Review

8 Describe how to evaluate the numerical expression.

$6 \times [(16 - 7) + (5 - 2)]$

_____

_____

_____

_____

9 Nicole has a cabinet in the shape of a right rectangular prism. The volume of the cabinet is 24 cubic feet. If the cabinet covers a floor space of 12 square feet, how tall is the cabinet?

_____

Name _____

Represent Fraction Sums and Differences

Draw a visual model to represent the situation. Then write an addition or subtraction equation to model the problem.

1 (MP) **Use Tools** Makayla refills the fuel for her portable heater before a camping trip. The fuel container has $\frac{1}{8}$ pound of fuel. She adds another $\frac{3}{4}$ pound of fuel. What equation represents the number of pounds of fuel in the container after she refills it?

_____

2 (MP) **Use Tools** Winding Pass is a long, steep trail. In the summer, $\frac{7}{10}$ of the hikers walk the entire trail. Of the same number of hikers in the winter, only $\frac{1}{5}$ walk the entire trail. What equation represents how many more hikers walk the entire trail in the summer than in the winter?

_____

3 **Financial Literacy** Audra budgets the money she earns from pet sitting. She budgets $\frac{1}{6}$ for art supplies and $\frac{1}{4}$ for savings. What equation represents the amount that Audra budgets for art supplies and savings?

_____

Test Prep

4 Zian hiked $\frac{2}{3}$ of the trails in a preserve last year. He hikes another $\frac{1}{4}$ of the trails this year. Which fraction strips represent the part of the trails Zian hiked?

5 Jamie spends $\frac{3}{5}$ hour doing homework. She spends $\frac{3}{10}$ hour doing chores. Which fraction strips represent how much more time Jamie spends doing homework?

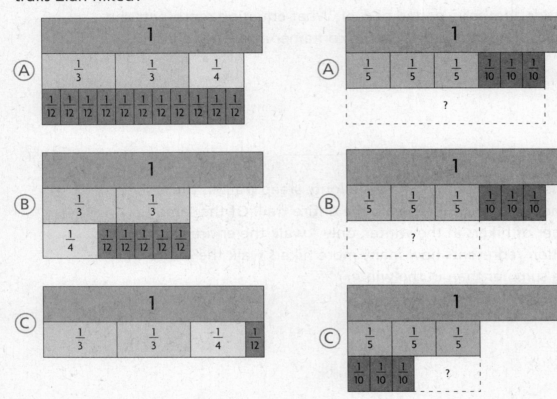

Spiral Review

6 What number is $\frac{1}{10}$ of 200? _____

7 Complete the equation and explain which properties you used.

$4 \times (3 \times 7) = 7 \times ($ _____ $\times 3)$

_____

_____

_____

Name _____

Represent Addition with Different-Sized Parts

1 (MP) **Use Structure** An obstacle course includes hurdles to jump over. For younger children, the hurdles have a height of $\frac{1}{2}$ yard. For older children, the hurdles are $\frac{1}{6}$ yard higher. What is the height of the hurdles for the older children? Draw a visual model to support your answer.

_____

(MP) **Use Tools** Use a visual model to find the sum.

2 $\frac{2}{3} + \frac{1}{12}$

3 $\frac{1}{5} + \frac{3}{10}$

_____

4 $\frac{5}{6} + \frac{1}{3}$

5 $\frac{5}{8} + \frac{1}{2}$

_____

6 **Math on the Spot** Maya makes trail mix by combining $\frac{1}{2}$ cup of mixed nuts, $\frac{1}{4}$ cup of dried fruit, and $\frac{1}{8}$ cup of chocolate morsels. What is the total amount of ingredients in her trail mix?

_____

7 (MP) **Use Tools** Shane combines $\frac{1}{2}$ liter of apple juice with $\frac{3}{10}$ liter of grape juice to make fruit punch. How much fruit punch does Shane make?

• Draw a visual model to represent the situation.

• How much fruit punch does Shane make?

_____

Test Prep

8 To train for an obstacle course, Marcus swims $\frac{1}{2}$ mile each day. Now he swims $\frac{3}{8}$ mile farther each day. How far does he swim each day now? Draw a visual model to support your answer.

_____

Use a visual model to find the sum.

9 $\frac{1}{2} + \frac{1}{5}$

Ⓐ $\frac{4}{5}$ Ⓒ $\frac{3}{5}$

Ⓑ $\frac{7}{10}$ Ⓓ $\frac{3}{10}$

10 $\frac{5}{6} + \frac{3}{4}$

Ⓐ $\frac{13}{12}$ Ⓒ $\frac{3}{2}$

Ⓑ $\frac{8}{6}$ Ⓓ $\frac{19}{12}$

Spiral Review

11 Mischa bakes 865 muffins. She packages 12 muffins in a box. How many boxes of 12 muffins does she package?

_____

12 Ricardo uses 1-centimeter cubes to build a tower. Write an expression for the volume of the tower. What is the volume?

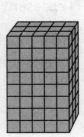

_____

LESSON 6.3
**More Practice/
Homework**

 ONLINE
Video Tutorials and
Interactive Examples

Represent Subtraction with Different-Sized Parts

1 (MP) **Use Tools** Devon wants to memorize $\frac{1}{2}$ of his lines for a play by the end of the week. He has already memorized $\frac{1}{8}$ of his lines. What fraction of his lines does he still have left to memorize? Draw a visual model to support your answer.

_____

(MP) **Use Tools** Use a visual model to find the difference.

2 $\frac{3}{8} - \frac{1}{4} =$ _____

3 $\frac{1}{2} - \frac{1}{5} =$ _____

4 $\frac{7}{6} - \frac{1}{2} =$ _____

5 $\frac{2}{3} - \frac{1}{6} =$ _____

6 **Math on the Spot** The picture at the right shows how much pizza was left over from lunch. Jason eats $\frac{1}{4}$ of the whole pizza for dinner. Write a fraction that represents the amount of pizza that is remaining after dinner.

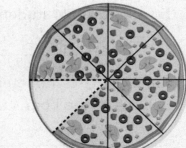

_____

Test Prep

7 Kendall puts four $\frac{1}{5}$-fraction strips in one row, and one $\frac{1}{10}$-fraction strip in the row below it. What is the difference in the lengths of these rows?

_____

8 Each actor in a play has to walk onstage at just the right time. Tonya walks onstage $\frac{1}{4}$ hour after the play starts. Jayla walks onstage $\frac{2}{3}$ hour after the play starts. How long after Tonya walks onstage does Jayla walk onstage? Draw a visual model to support your answer.

_____

Use a visual model to find the difference.

9 $\frac{5}{6} - \frac{1}{12} = \blacksquare$

   Ⓐ $\frac{4}{12}$ Ⓑ $\frac{3}{6}$ Ⓒ $\frac{4}{6}$ Ⓓ $\frac{9}{12}$

10 $\frac{1}{2} - \frac{1}{5} = \blacksquare$

   Ⓐ $\frac{1}{10}$ Ⓑ $\frac{1}{5}$ Ⓒ $\frac{3}{10}$ Ⓓ $\frac{2}{5}$

Spiral Review

11 A school needs buses to take 105 students on a field trip. If each bus can take 24 students, how many buses does the school need?

_____

12 Jamil uses 1-centimeter cubes to build a box. What is the volume of the box?

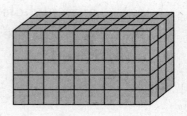

_____

Rewrite Fractions with a Common Denominator

1 **(MP) Reason** Luis reads about two popular cell phone apps. One app uses $\frac{1}{2}$ of a phone's storage space. The other app uses $\frac{5}{12}$ of a phone's storage space. Explain how Luis can find the difference in the storage space of the two apps without drawing a visual model.

_____

_____

_____

_____

_____

Use a common denominator to write equivalent fractions.

2 $\frac{1}{4}, \frac{2}{3}$

3 $\frac{11}{12}, \frac{1}{4}$

4 $\frac{1}{3}, \frac{4}{5}$

_____   _____   _____

5 $\frac{3}{5}, \frac{1}{3}$

6 $\frac{5}{6}, \frac{1}{12}$

7 $\frac{7}{8}, \frac{2}{3}$

_____   _____   _____

8 **Math on the Spot** Arnold had three pieces of different color string all the same length. Arnold cut the blue string into 2 equal-sized lengths. He cut the red string into 5 equal-sized lengths, and the green string into 10 equal-sized lengths. He needs to cut the string so each color has the same number of equal-sized lengths. What is the least number of equal-sized lengths each color string could have?

_____

Test Prep

9 Select all common denominators that can be used to write equivalent fractions for $\frac{3}{4}$ and $\frac{5}{8}$.

(A) 4   (B) 8   (C) 12   (D) 16   (E) 24

10 Kai asks the students in her class to vote on places they would like to visit. In the class, $\frac{3}{20}$ vote for a large city, $\frac{3}{5}$ vote for the beach, and $\frac{1}{4}$ vote for the mountains. Write a numerical expression using equivalent fractions with a common denominator to model the part of the class that would like to visit these places.

_____

11 Use a common denominator to rewrite $\frac{7}{10}$ and $\frac{8}{15}$.

_____

12 Which fraction pair shows the fractions $\frac{5}{12}$ and $\frac{3}{8}$ expressed with a common denominator?

(A) $\frac{5}{24}$ and $\frac{3}{24}$ (B) $\frac{40}{96}$ and $\frac{36}{96}$ (C) $\frac{20}{48}$ and $\frac{12}{48}$ (D) $\frac{15}{36}$ and $\frac{12}{36}$

Spiral Review

13 A baseball league has 176 baseball players divided equally into 16 teams. How many players are on each team?

_____

14 Arun travels 24 miles each hour on a 102-mile bike trip. How many hours does the bike trip take?

_____

15 Jorge uses centimeter cubes to build the right rectangular prism with no gaps or overlaps. Describe how Jorge can find the volume of the prism.

_____

_____

_____

Name _____

Use Benchmarks and Number Sense to Estimate

1 (MP) **Use Tools** The number lines show the points $\frac{3}{8}$ and $1\frac{4}{5}$.

$\frac{0}{8}$ $\frac{1}{8}$ $\frac{2}{8}$ $\frac{3}{8}$ $\frac{4}{8}$ $\frac{5}{8}$ $\frac{6}{8}$ $\frac{7}{8}$ $\frac{8}{8}$ $1\frac{1}{8}$ $1\frac{2}{8}$ $1\frac{3}{8}$ $1\frac{4}{8}$ $1\frac{5}{8}$ $1\frac{6}{8}$ $1\frac{7}{8}$ $1\frac{8}{8}$

0    $\frac{1}{2}$ 1 $1\frac{1}{2}$ 2

$\frac{0}{5}$ $\frac{1}{5}$ $\frac{2}{5}$ $\frac{3}{5}$ $\frac{4}{5}$ $\frac{5}{5}$ $1\frac{1}{5}$ $1\frac{2}{5}$ $1\frac{3}{5}$ $1\frac{4}{5}$ $1\frac{5}{5}$

0    $\frac{1}{2}$ 1 $1\frac{1}{2}$ 2

Use benchmarks to estimate the sum $\frac{3}{8} + 1\frac{4}{5}$.

_____

2 (MP) **Use Structure** Estimate to determine whether $2\frac{2}{3} - \frac{9}{10}$ or $\frac{5}{6} + \frac{1}{5}$ is greater. Explain your choice.

_____

_____

Use benchmarks to estimate the sum or difference.

3 $\frac{11}{12} + \frac{2}{5}$ _____

4 $1\frac{1}{10} - \frac{5}{8}$ _____

5 (MP) **Use Structure** Estimate the sums.

• $3\frac{2}{10} + 1\frac{1}{6}$ _____ $1\frac{4}{5} + 1\frac{7}{8}$ _____

• Which is the lesser sum? Explain.

_____

_____

6 Darlene runs $\frac{6}{10}$ kilometer in the morning and $1\frac{2}{5}$ kilometers in the afternoon. About how many kilometers does Darlene run?

_____

Test Prep

7 Mario wants to mail three books with the following weights: $\frac{5}{8}$ pound, $\frac{7}{16}$ pound, and $\frac{3}{4}$ pound. Can Mario mail the books in a box that can hold up to $2\frac{1}{2}$ pounds? Use benchmarks to justify your answer.

_____

_____

8 The distance from Will's house to a park is $1\frac{9}{10}$ miles. Will leaves his house and walks $\frac{2}{5}$ mile toward the park. About how much farther does he have to walk to reach the park?

_____

9 Beth buys $2\frac{7}{8}$ ounces of cinnamon. She pours the cinnamon into a jar that already contains $3\frac{1}{4}$ ounces of cinnamon. About how many ounces of cinnamon are in the jar?

_____

10 Which sum or difference could have an estimate of 2? Select all that apply.

(A) $1\frac{8}{10} + \frac{1}{8}$

(B) $2\frac{1}{6} - \frac{1}{10}$

(C) $1\frac{7}{16} + 1\frac{7}{8}$

(D) $2\frac{2}{3} - 1\frac{3}{4}$

(E) $1\frac{1}{5} + 1\frac{1}{4}$

Spiral Review

11 The printer in the office can print 74 pages in one minute. About how long would it take to print 1,392 pages?

_____

12 Jessa is setting up for the awards dinner. There are 216 people coming to the dinner, and 12 people can sit at each table. How many tables does Jessa need to set up?

_____

Assess Reasonableness of Fraction Sums and Differences

1 Charlotte uses two boards to build a tabletop. How wide is the tabletop?

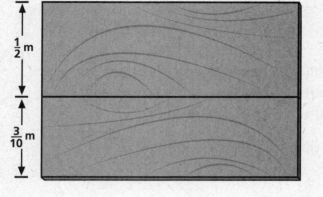

$\frac{1}{2}$ m

$\frac{3}{10}$ m

2 (MP) **Reason** Hugo walks $\frac{5}{6}$ mile from his home to the library on Monday. He walks $\frac{1}{3}$ mile from his home to the park on Tuesday.

- How much farther does he walk on Monday than on Tuesday?

_____

- Is your answer reasonable? Explain.

_____

Write the expression using fractions with a common denominator. Then find the sum or difference.

3 $\frac{3}{4} - \frac{1}{3}$

_____

4 $\frac{2}{5} + \frac{1}{2}$

_____

Find the sum or difference.

5 $\frac{2}{8} + \frac{11}{16}$

_____

6 $\frac{9}{10} - \frac{3}{5}$

_____

Test Prep

7 What is the value of the expression $\frac{5}{8} + \frac{1}{4}$?

(A) $\frac{6}{12}$ (B) $\frac{6}{8}$ (C) $\frac{7}{8}$ (D) 1

8 What is the value of the expression $\frac{10}{12} - \frac{3}{6}$?

(A) $\frac{1}{6}$ (B) $\frac{4}{12}$ (C) $\frac{7}{12}$ (D) $\frac{7}{6}$

9 Sonny is writing a report on the solar system. He spends $\frac{3}{5}$ hour researching facts about the planets. He spends $\frac{1}{3}$ hour drawing some planets.

- Write an expression that models the time Sonny spends on his report.

_____

- How much time does Sonny spend on his report?

_____

- Is your answer reasonable? Explain.

_____

_____

_____

10 Select all the expressions equivalent to $\frac{7}{10}$.

(A) $\frac{8}{10} - \frac{1}{5}$

(B) $\frac{1}{5} + \frac{1}{2}$

(C) $\frac{5}{10} + \frac{1}{4}$

(D) $\frac{10}{10} - \frac{3}{10}$

(E) $\frac{1}{2} + \frac{1}{10} + \frac{1}{10}$

Spiral Review

11 Divide. Use partial quotients.

$827 \div 24$ _____

$1,872 \div 13$ _____

12 Divide.

$540 \div 12$ _____

$168 \div 14$ _____

Name _____

Assess Reasonableness of Mixed Number Sums and Differences

1 (MP) **Attend to Precision** Denise needs 4 pounds of soil to fill a flowerpot. She has a bag with $2\frac{1}{8}$ pounds of soil and a box with $1\frac{3}{4}$ pounds of soil. Does Denise have enough soil to fill the flowerpot? Explain.

_____

_____

_____

Find the sum or difference.

2 $1\frac{1}{3} + 2\frac{3}{5}$

_____

3 $6\frac{1}{2} - 2\frac{1}{8}$

_____

4 $4\frac{5}{6} - 1\frac{1}{2}$

_____

5 $3\frac{1}{5} + 2\frac{1}{4}$

_____

6 **Math on the Spot** Gavin needs to make 2 batches of Sunrise Orange paint. Explain how you could find the total amount of paint Gavin mixed.

_____

_____

_____

_____

_____

Paint Gavin Uses (in ounces)		
Red	Yellow	Shade
$2\frac{5}{8}$	$3\frac{1}{4}$	Sunrise Orange
$3\frac{9}{10}$	$2\frac{3}{8}$	Tangerine
$5\frac{5}{6}$	$5\frac{5}{6}$	Mango

© Houghton Mifflin Harcourt Publishing Company

Test Prep

7 What is the value of the expression $3\frac{5}{6} - 1\frac{1}{3}$?

Ⓐ $1\frac{3}{6}$ Ⓑ $1\frac{4}{6}$ Ⓒ $2\frac{1}{3}$ Ⓓ $2\frac{3}{6}$

8 What is the value of the expression $2\frac{2}{5} + 1\frac{1}{3}$?

Ⓐ $3\frac{11}{15}$ Ⓑ $3\frac{3}{8}$ Ⓒ $3\frac{3}{8}$ Ⓓ $3\frac{3}{15}$

9 Lara jumps rope for $2\frac{3}{4}$ minutes. Then she does squats for $1\frac{1}{2}$ minutes. How many minutes does Lara spend jumping rope and doing squats? Is your answer reasonable? Explain.

_____

_____

10 Select all expressions equivalent to $2\frac{5}{12}$.

Ⓐ $1\frac{1}{4} + 1\frac{2}{12}$

Ⓑ $4\frac{3}{4} - 2\frac{1}{3}$

Ⓒ $1\frac{3}{6} + 1\frac{1}{2}$

Ⓓ $5\frac{7}{12} - 3\frac{1}{6}$

Ⓔ $1\frac{1}{12} + 1\frac{2}{3}$

11 What is the value of the expression $6\frac{7}{8} - 2\frac{3}{4}$? _____

Spiral Review

12 Alisha is making sandwiches for her graduation party. She cuts each sandwich into 4 equal pieces. If there are 125 people coming to the party, how many sandwiches does Alisha have to make so that everyone gets one piece?

_____

13 George has 314 bugs in his bug collection book. Each page in the book holds 16 bugs. How many pages does George use to show all of his bugs?

_____

Name _____

LESSON 7.4
More Practice/ Homework

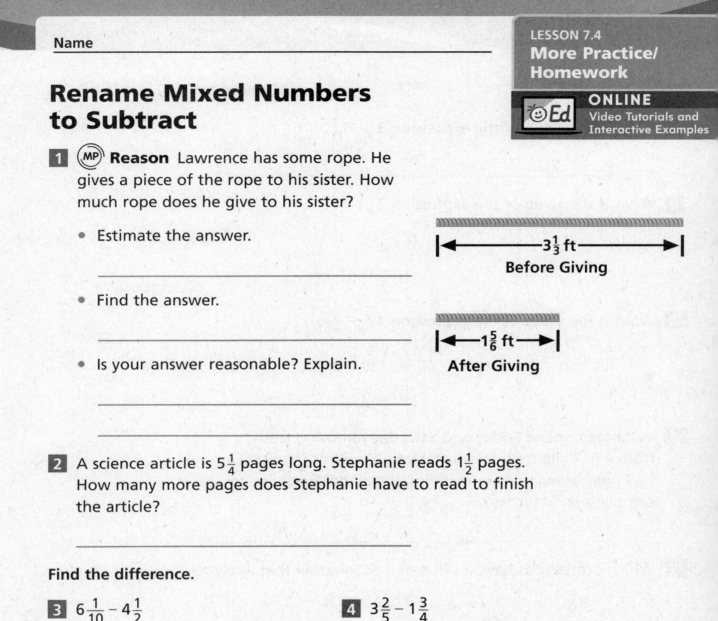
ONLINE
Video Tutorials and
Interactive Examples

Rename Mixed Numbers to Subtract

1 (MP) **Reason** Lawrence has some rope. He gives a piece of the rope to his sister. How much rope does he give to his sister?

- Estimate the answer.

  _____

- Find the answer.

  _____

- Is your answer reasonable? Explain.

  _____

  _____

$\overset{\longleftarrow\!\!\!\!—3\tfrac{1}{3}\text{ ft}—\!\!\!\!\longrightarrow}{}$
Before Giving

$\overset{\longleftarrow\!1\tfrac{5}{6}\text{ ft}\!\longrightarrow}{}$
After Giving

2 A science article is $5\tfrac{1}{4}$ pages long. Stephanie reads $1\tfrac{1}{2}$ pages. How many more pages does Stephanie have to read to finish the article?

_____

Find the difference.

3 $6\tfrac{1}{10} - 4\tfrac{1}{2}$

_____

4 $3\tfrac{2}{5} - 1\tfrac{3}{4}$

_____

5 $2\tfrac{2}{3} - 1\tfrac{8}{9}$

_____

6 $6\tfrac{1}{2} - 3\tfrac{6}{8}$

_____

7 **Math on the Spot** A roller coaster has 3 trains with 7 rows on each train. Riders stand in rows of 6, for a total of 42 riders on each train. The operators of the coaster recorded the number of riders on each train during a run. In the first train, $6\tfrac{1}{6}$ rows were filled. On the second train, all 7 rows were filled. On the third train, $4\tfrac{1}{2}$ rows were filled. How many rows were empty on the first train?

_____

Test Prep

8 What is the value of the expression $3\frac{1}{3} - 1\frac{3}{5}$?

_____

9 What is the value of the expression $2\frac{1}{8} - 1\frac{1}{2}$?

Ⓐ $1\frac{1}{8}$ Ⓒ $\frac{5}{8}$

Ⓑ $\frac{7}{8}$ Ⓓ $\frac{1}{2}$

10 What is the value of the expression $4\frac{3}{10} - 2\frac{4}{5}$?

Ⓐ $1\frac{5}{10}$ Ⓒ $1\frac{9}{10}$

Ⓑ $1\frac{4}{5}$ Ⓓ $2\frac{5}{10}$

11 Volunteers spend Friday and Saturday removing trash from a $6\frac{2}{5}$-mile trail. They complete $4\frac{7}{8}$ miles of the trail on Friday. How many more miles of trail do they need to complete on Saturday?

_____

12 Which expressions have a value of $1\frac{2}{6}$? Select all that apply.

Ⓐ $5\frac{1}{3} - 3\frac{1}{2}$

Ⓑ $4\frac{1}{6} - 3\frac{1}{3}$

Ⓒ $3\frac{1}{2} - 1\frac{7}{6}$

Ⓓ $6 - 4\frac{2}{3}$

Ⓔ $3\frac{1}{6} - 1\frac{1}{2}$

Spiral Review

13 Divide. Use partial quotients.

$1,398 \div 15$ _____

$924 \div 12$ _____

14 Use a visual model to find the sum.

$\frac{1}{6} + \frac{3}{12}$ _____

Apply Properties of Addition

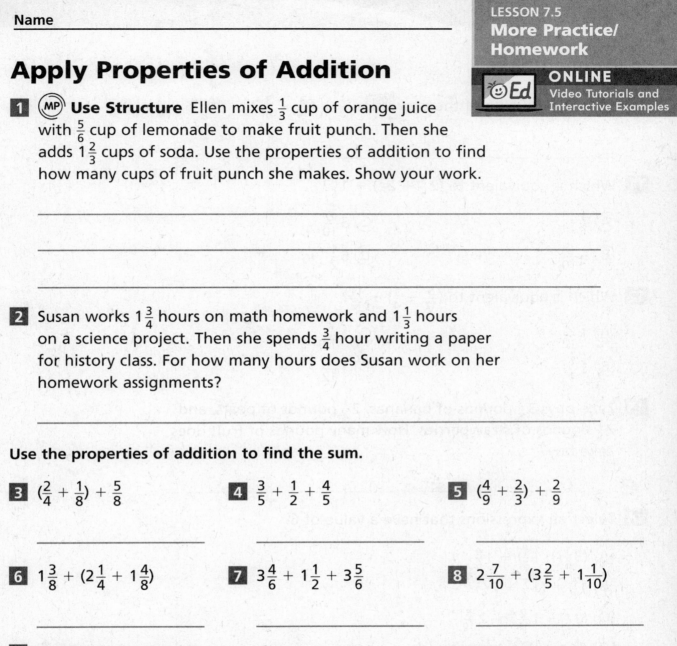
1 (MP) **Use Structure** Ellen mixes $\frac{1}{3}$ cup of orange juice with $\frac{5}{6}$ cup of lemonade to make fruit punch. Then she adds $1\frac{2}{3}$ cups of soda. Use the properties of addition to find how many cups of fruit punch she makes. Show your work.

_____

_____

_____

2 Susan works $1\frac{3}{4}$ hours on math homework and $1\frac{1}{3}$ hours on a science project. Then she spends $\frac{3}{4}$ hour writing a paper for history class. For how many hours does Susan work on her homework assignments?

_____

Use the properties of addition to find the sum.

3 $(\frac{2}{4} + \frac{1}{8}) + \frac{5}{8}$

4 $\frac{3}{5} + \frac{1}{2} + \frac{4}{5}$

5 $(\frac{4}{9} + \frac{2}{3}) + \frac{2}{9}$

_____ _____ _____

6 $1\frac{3}{8} + (2\frac{1}{4} + 1\frac{4}{8})$

7 $3\frac{4}{6} + 1\frac{1}{2} + 3\frac{5}{6}$

8 $2\frac{7}{10} + (3\frac{2}{5} + 1\frac{1}{10})$

_____ _____ _____

9 **Math on the Spot** On one afternoon, Mario walks from his school to the mall. That evening, Mario walks from the mall to the library and then to his home. Describe how you can use the properties to find how far Mario walks.

Sports Complex

School

$\frac{2}{3}$ mile

Park

Mall $\frac{2}{5}$ mile

Kyle's Home

$\frac{2}{3}$ mile

$\frac{4}{5}$ mile

$1\frac{1}{3}$ miles

Library

Mario's Home

$1\frac{3}{5}$ miles

_____

_____

_____

_____

Test Prep

10 What is the value of the expression $\frac{7}{8} + (\frac{3}{16} + \frac{3}{8})$?

_____

11 Which is equivalent to $(2\frac{3}{5} + 2\frac{1}{2}) + 1\frac{4}{5}$?

Ⓐ 7

Ⓑ $6\frac{9}{10}$

Ⓒ $6\frac{6}{10}$

Ⓓ $6\frac{1}{2}$

12 Which is equivalent to $(\frac{5}{12} + \frac{1}{4}) + \frac{11}{12}$?

Ⓐ $1\frac{2}{12}$

Ⓑ $1\frac{1}{4}$

Ⓒ $1\frac{6}{12}$

Ⓓ $1\frac{7}{12}$

13 Zeke buys $3\frac{5}{8}$ pounds of bananas, $2\frac{1}{4}$ pounds of pears, and $2\frac{7}{8}$ pounds of strawberries. How many pounds of fruit does Zeke buy?

_____

14 Select all expressions that have a value of 6.

Ⓐ $(3\frac{1}{6} + 1\frac{1}{3}) + 1\frac{4}{6}$

Ⓑ $1\frac{5}{8} + (1\frac{1}{2} + 2\frac{7}{8})$

Ⓒ $(2\frac{1}{2} + 1\frac{2}{10}) + 2\frac{3}{10}$

Ⓓ $(\frac{4}{5} + 4\frac{1}{3}) + 1\frac{2}{5}$

Ⓔ $2\frac{1}{8} + (2\frac{1}{2} + 1\frac{3}{8})$

Spiral Review

15 Write an expression to model the description.

Four times as much as the difference of 74 and 13

_____

16 Find the sum or difference.

$\frac{1}{4} + \frac{5}{12} =$ _____

$\frac{3}{4} - \frac{1}{6} =$ _____

LESSON 7.6
**More Practice/
Homework**

ONLINE
Video Tutorials and
Interactive Examples

Practice Addition and Subtraction Using Equations

1 (MP) **Reason** One balloon is $3\frac{7}{10}$ meters above the ground. A second balloon is $2\frac{3}{5}$ meters higher. How far above the ground is the second balloon?

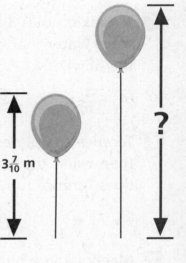

$3\frac{7}{10}$ m

- Write an addition equation and a related subtraction equation to model the problem. Use *b* to represent the height of the second balloon.

  _____

- Estimate the answer.

  _____

- How far above the ground is the second balloon?

  _____

- Is your answer reasonable? Explain.

  _____

  _____

2 (MP) **Model with Mathematics** Nelly watched two movies on Saturday. The second movie lasted $2\frac{3}{4}$ hours. Nelly spent $5\frac{1}{3}$ hours watching both movies. How long was the first movie?

- Write an addition equation and a related subtraction equation to model the problem.

  _____

- How long was the first movie?

  _____

  _____

3 (MP) **Model with Mathematics** Beth's summer vacation lasted $12\frac{3}{7}$ weeks. At the beginning of her vacation, she spent some time at soccer camp and $2\frac{4}{7}$ weeks at her grandmother's home. She then had $6\frac{6}{7}$ weeks of vacation remaining. Write an equation to model this situation. How many weeks did Beth spend at soccer camp?

_____

Test Prep

4 Ms. Li stores flour in a jar. She buys $2\frac{7}{8}$ pounds of flour and puts it in the jar. Now the jar holds $4\frac{1}{2}$ pounds of flour. How much flour was in the jar before Ms. Li's purchase?

(A) $2\frac{1}{8}$ lb   (B) $1\frac{7}{8}$ lb   (C) $1\frac{5}{8}$ lb   (D) $1\frac{1}{2}$ lb

5 A beaker holds $3\frac{9}{10}$ liters of water. A bowl holds $2\frac{1}{2}$ liters more water than the beaker. How much water is in the bowl?

(A) $6\frac{4}{10}$ L   (B) $6\frac{3}{10}$ L   (C) $6\frac{1}{5}$ L   (D) 6 L

6 Terence completes 9 laps around a track. He runs some laps, then walks the last $1\frac{3}{4}$ laps to cool down. How many laps does Terence run?

(A) $7\frac{1}{4}$ (B) $7\frac{3}{4}$ (C) $8\frac{1}{4}$ (D) $10\frac{3}{4}$

7 Maeko buys a birdfeeder that can hold $3\frac{1}{2}$ pounds of sunflower seeds. She has $1\frac{9}{16}$ pounds of sunflower seeds. How many more pounds of sunflowers seeds does Maeko need to fill the feeder?

_____

8 Roberto measures his pencil to be $2\frac{5}{8}$ inches long. His friend Hakim's pencil is $1\frac{1}{2}$ inches longer than Roberto's pencil. Write an addition equation and a related subtraction equation to model the problem. How long is Hakim's pencil?

_____

Spiral Review

9 Evaluate the numerical expression.

$$35 - 5 \times (12 - 7)$$

_____

10 Jackie works $\frac{2}{3}$ hour on a science project. Lucas works $\frac{3}{4}$ hour on the project. How much longer does Lucas work on the project than Jackie?

_____

Explore Groups of Equal Shares to Show Multiplication

1 (MP) **Attend to Precision** Vanessa has 24 marbles. She gives $\frac{3}{8}$ of the marbles to her brother Cisco.

- If you divide Vanessa's marbles into 8 equal groups, how many are in each group? _____

- How many marbles does Vanessa give to Cisco? Explain.

_____

_____

Draw a visual model to solve.

2 $\frac{1}{6}$ of 18

_____

3 When Fran began training to become a professional swimmer, she could swim only $\frac{2}{3}$ of the number of laps she can now swim in a session. If Fran can now swim 48 laps in a session, how many laps did she swim in a session when she began?

_____

4 **Math on the Spot** Zack, Teri, and Paco combined the foreign stamps from their collections for a stamp show. Out of their collections, $\frac{4}{7}$ of Zack's stamps, $\frac{3}{4}$ of Teri's stamps, and $\frac{3}{11}$ of Paco's stamps were from foreign countries. How many stamps were in their display? Explain how you solved the problem.

Stamps Collected	
Name	**Number of Stamps**
Zack	28
Teri	16
Paco	22

_____

_____

_____

Test Prep

5 A bookstore has 52 books about gardening. Three-fourths of the books are paperbacks. How many paperback books about gardening does the store have?

(A) 13

(B) 18

(C) 34

(D) 39

6 Which is $\frac{1}{7}$ of 42?

(A) 6

(B) 7

(C) 36

(D) 298

7 Find $\frac{1}{9}$ of 63.

_____

8 Hector originally had $60 in his bank account. After buying some books, Hector now has $\frac{3}{10}$ of the original $60. How much does Hector now have in his bank account?

_____

9 A bag has 32 cups of flour. Miriam uses $\frac{5}{8}$ of the flour to bake bread. How many cups of flour are left in the bag?

_____

Spiral Review

10 Use the benchmarks 0, $\frac{1}{2}$, and 1 to estimate the sum.

$\frac{4}{6} + \frac{2}{5}$

11 The copier makes 86 copies in one minute. How long will it take to make 2,752 copies?

Represent Multiplication of Whole Numbers by Fractions

 ONLINE
Video Tutorials and
Interactive Examples

1 (MP) **Critique Reasoning** Barbara picked 36 apples. She needs to put $\frac{2}{9}$ of the apples in a basket. Barbara says she will put 12 apples in the basket. Is Barbara correct? Explain.

_____

_____

Draw a visual model to find the product.

2 $\frac{2}{5} \times 10 =$ _____

3 **Open Ended** Write a story context for the equation shown.

$$\frac{3}{7} \times 28 = 12$$

_____

_____

_____

4 (MP) **Reason** Tarique drew a visual model to show the product $\frac{2}{5} \times 7$. How could you change the visual model to show the product $\frac{28}{5}$? Explain and write an equation.

_____

_____

_____

_____

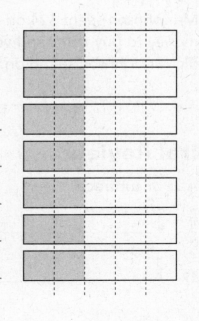

Test Prep

5 A store has a display of 42 bottles. Four-sevenths of the bottles are green. How many of the bottles in the display are green?

- (A) 6
- (B) 18
- (C) 24
- (D) 28

6 Which is the product $\frac{2}{3} \times 45$?

- (A) 15
- (B) 30
- (C) 68
- (D) 90

7 What is the product $\frac{3}{5} \times 60$?

_____

8 Nina makes 60 slices of pizza for a party. At the party, $\frac{7}{12}$ of the slices are eaten. How many slices are left?

_____

9 Mr. Johnson spent $24 on groceries. He used $\frac{5}{8}$ of the money to buy fruits and vegetables. How much money did Mr. Johnson spend on fruits and vegetables?

_____

Spiral Review

10 Add or subtract.

$\frac{2}{3} + \frac{3}{9}$ _____

$\frac{7}{12} - \frac{1}{6}$ _____

11 Divide. Use partial quotients.

$824 \div 22$ _____

$1,488 \div 12$ _____

© Houghton Mifflin Harcourt Publishing Company

Represent Multiplication with Unit Fractions

1 (MP) **Attend to Precision** A juice shop has different sizes of drinks. The regular-sized drink is $\frac{1}{3}$ of the size of the super-sized drink. The mini-sized drink is $\frac{1}{5}$ of the size of the regular-sized drink.

- Into how many drinks would you divide a

  super-sized drink to show $\frac{1}{3}$? _____

- Into how many drinks would you divide a

  regular-sized drink to show $\frac{1}{5}$? _____

- What fraction of the super-sized drink is the

  mini-sized drink? _____

Draw a visual model to find the product.

2 $\frac{1}{2} \times \frac{1}{6} =$ _____

3 (MP) **Model with Mathematics** Enzo has a block of clay. He cuts off $\frac{1}{4}$ of the block to make a bowl. Then he realizes he has too much clay and uses $\frac{1}{6}$ of this piece to make his bowl. How much of the original block of clay does Enzo use to make his bowl? Write an equation to model the problem.

_____

4 (MP) **Reason** An internet company spends half their yearly profits on advertising for the next year. Of the remaining half, they spend $\frac{1}{5}$ on new computers. What fraction of the total profits does the company spend on new computers? Use the number line to show how you can find the fraction.

_____

$\longleftarrow\mid\hspace{3cm}\mid\longrightarrow$

     0   1

Test Prep

5 Multiply $\frac{1}{7} \times \frac{1}{4}$.

Ⓐ $\frac{1}{28}$

Ⓑ $\frac{1}{24}$

Ⓒ $\frac{1}{11}$

Ⓓ $\frac{4}{7}$

6 Select all the expressions that equal $\frac{1}{24}$.

Ⓐ $\frac{1}{12} \times \frac{1}{4}$

Ⓑ $\frac{1}{8} \times \frac{1}{3}$

Ⓒ $\frac{1}{4} \times \frac{1}{6}$

Ⓓ $\frac{1}{3} \times \frac{1}{9}$

Ⓔ $\frac{1}{2} \times \frac{1}{12}$

7 Multiply $\frac{1}{9} \times \frac{1}{7}$.

_____

8 Ahmed has a large can of applesauce. He gives $\frac{1}{3}$ of the applesauce to Sasha. Sasha uses $\frac{1}{10}$ of the applesauce to bake muffins. How much of the original container of applesauce does Sasha use to bake muffins?

_____

Spiral Review

9 Add or subtract using a common denominator.

$3\frac{1}{6} + 4\frac{1}{2} =$ _____

$3\frac{1}{4} - 1\frac{2}{3} =$ _____

10 Add.

$\frac{2}{4} + \frac{3}{12} =$ _____

$\frac{2}{6} + \frac{1}{4} =$ _____

LESSON 8.4
**More Practice/
Homework**

ONLINE
Video Tutorials and
Interactive Examples

Represent Multiplication of Fractions

1 (MP) **Model with Mathematics** Dominick's doctor tells him to take a one-half dose of medicine. One dose equals $\frac{2}{3}$ tablespoon. Draw a visual model to find the amount of medicine Dominick needs. Write an equation to model the problem. How many tablespoons is a one-half dose?

_____

2 (MP) **Use Tools** A parking lot is $\frac{7}{9}$ full of vehicles. Of these vehicles, $\frac{5}{7}$ are compact cars. The parking lot owner needs to know what fraction of the total space is used by compact cars.

• Draw a visual model to represent the problem.

• Write an equation to model the problem.

_____

• What fraction of the whole parking lot is used by compact cars?

_____

Draw a visual model to solve.

3 $\frac{3}{8} \times \frac{8}{11}$

_____

Test Prep

4 A toy designer makes a miniature version of the vehicle shown. The height of the miniature version is $\frac{5}{12}$ of the height of the original vehicle. What is the height of the miniature version?

$\frac{3}{5}$ m

Ⓐ $\frac{3}{12}$ meter   Ⓒ $\frac{12}{5}$ meters

Ⓑ $\frac{5}{12}$ meter   Ⓓ $\frac{12}{3}$ meters

5 Aubrey's little sister is $\frac{6}{8}$ yard tall. When Aubrey was the same age, she was $\frac{5}{6}$ of the height of her little sister. How tall was Aubrey when she was her little sister's age?

_____

6 Select all the expressions that have a value of $\frac{4}{6}$.

Ⓐ $\frac{4}{5} \times \frac{5}{6}$ Ⓑ $\frac{2}{3} \times \frac{3}{4}$ Ⓒ $\frac{1}{2} \times \frac{2}{3}$ Ⓓ $\frac{3}{4} \times \frac{2}{3}$ Ⓔ $\frac{5}{6} \times \frac{4}{5}$

7 Use the number line to find $\frac{4}{5} \times \frac{5}{8}$.

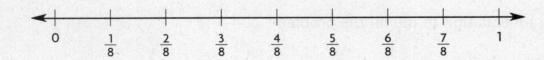

0   $\frac{1}{8}$ $\frac{2}{8}$ $\frac{3}{8}$ $\frac{4}{8}$ $\frac{5}{8}$ $\frac{6}{8}$ $\frac{7}{8}$ 1

Spiral Review

8 Bruce has a piece of rope that is $8\frac{3}{8}$ feet long. He cuts off a section that is $4\frac{1}{4}$ feet long. How much rope does he have left?

_____

9 Mr. Melnikov has 336 coins in his coin collection book. Each page in the book holds 24 coins. How many pages does Mr. Melnikov need to show all of his coins?

_____

LESSON 8.5
**More Practice/
Homework**

ONLINE
Video Tutorials and
Interactive Examples

Use Representations of Area to Develop Procedures

1 (MP) **Attend to Precision** Of all the cookies in a cookie jar, $\frac{4}{5}$ are oatmeal. Of the oatmeal cookies, $\frac{2}{3}$ have nuts. What fraction of all the cookies in the cookie jar are oatmeal with nuts?

_____

2 (MP) **Use Tools** The dimensions of a patch are shown. What is the area of the patch?

• Use the square to help you find the area.

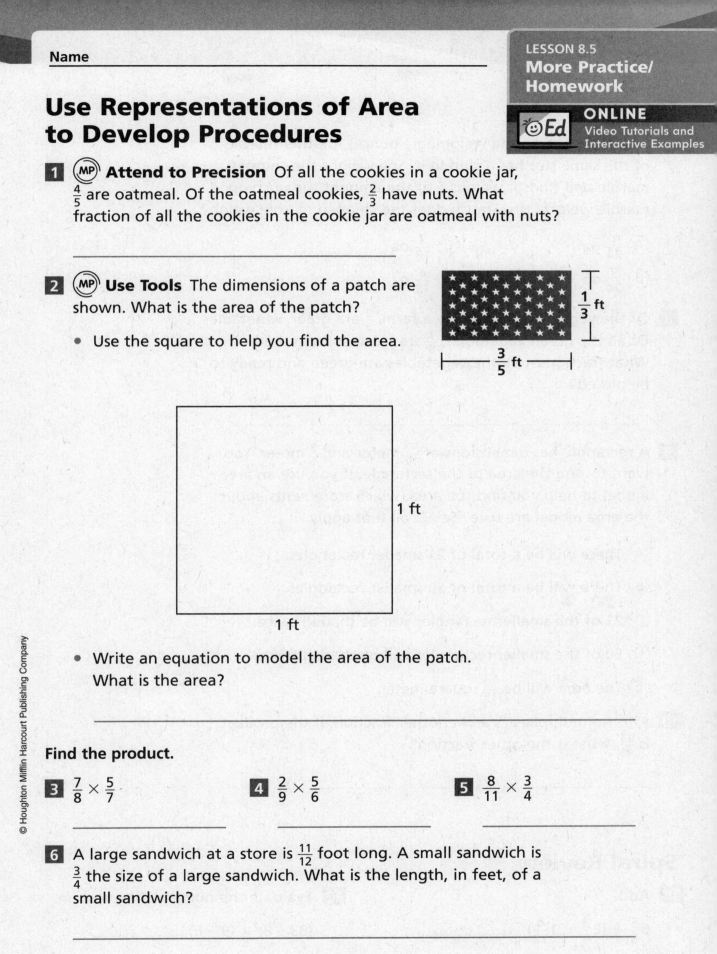

1 ft

1 ft

$\frac{1}{3}$ ft

$\frac{3}{5}$ ft

• Write an equation to model the area of the patch. What is the area?

_____

Find the product.

3 $\frac{7}{8} \times \frac{5}{7}$

4 $\frac{2}{9} \times \frac{5}{6}$

5 $\frac{8}{11} \times \frac{3}{4}$

_____

6 A large sandwich at a store is $\frac{11}{12}$ foot long. A small sandwich is $\frac{3}{4}$ the size of a large sandwich. What is the length, in feet, of a small sandwich?

_____

Test Prep

7 Matilda has a marble weighing $\frac{1}{6}$ ounce. Another marble of the same size has a chip in it. She weighs the chipped marble and finds it weighs $\frac{3}{4}$ of the amount the unchipped marble weighs. How much does the chipped marble weigh?

Ⓐ $\frac{1}{24}$ oz

Ⓒ $\frac{3}{18}$ oz

Ⓑ $\frac{3}{24}$ oz

Ⓓ $\frac{4}{18}$ oz

8 Of the vegetables grown on a farm, $\frac{2}{3}$ are green vegetables. Of all the green vegetables, $\frac{7}{8}$ are ready to be picked. What fraction of all the vegetables are green and ready to be picked?

_____

9 A rectangle has dimensions of $\frac{7}{10}$ meter and $\frac{3}{5}$ meter. You want to find the area of the rectangle. If you use an area model to help you find the area, which statements about the area model are true? Select all that apply.

Ⓐ There will be a total of 21 smaller rectangles.

Ⓑ There will be a total of 50 smaller rectangles.

Ⓒ 21 of the smaller rectangles will be shaded twice.

Ⓓ 50 of the smaller rectangles will be shaded twice.

Ⓔ The area will be $\frac{10}{15}$ square meter.

10 Alfonso multiplies $\frac{5}{12}$ and another fraction. If the product is $\frac{15}{48}$, what is the other fraction?

_____

Spiral Review

11 Add.

$6\frac{5}{8} + (2\frac{3}{8} + 1\frac{4}{12})$ _____

12 Evaluate the numerical expression.

$(33 - 8) \times (9 - 6)$ _____

Interpret Fraction Multiplication as Scaling

1 **STEM** An elephant's skeleton has about 345 bones. At birth, a human skeleton has about $\frac{3}{5} \times 345$ bones. Which has more bones, an elephant or a human? Explain.

_____

2 (MP) **Use Tools** Use a number line to help you answer the questions.

- Where is the product $\frac{5}{12} \times \frac{11}{20}$ located on the number line in relation to $\frac{11}{20}$? Why?

_____

- Where is the product $\frac{12}{12} \times \frac{11}{20}$ located on the number line in relation to $\frac{11}{20}$? Why?

_____

The length of Florida's Seven Mile Bridge is rescaled as modeled by the expressions shown in 3–5. Use *shorter*, *longer*, or *same* to describe how the length of the rescaled bridge compares to the actual length of Florida's Seven Mile Bridge.

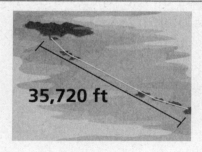

35,720 ft

3 $\frac{27}{20} \times 35,720$ **4** $\frac{9}{20} \times 35,720$ **5** $\frac{20}{20} \times 35,720$

_____   _____   _____

6 (MP) **Construct Arguments** A stegosaurus dinosaur is about $\frac{15}{12}$ as tall as an ankylosaurus. A stokesosaurus dinosaur is about $\frac{8}{12}$ as tall as an ankylosaurus. The ankylosaurus is about 11 feet tall. Which dinosaur is the tallest? Shortest? Explain.

_____

_____

_____

_____

Test Prep

7 In 2016, the number of tigers in the wild was about $\frac{16}{13}$ of the number of tigers in the wild in 2010. Which statement is true?

Ⓐ The number of wild tigers decreased from 2010 to 2016.

Ⓑ The number of wild tigers in 2016 was the same as the number in 2010.

Ⓒ The number of wild tigers increased from 2010 to 2016.

Ⓓ A population comparison between the two years cannot be made.

8 Write *equal to*, *greater than*, or *less than*.

The product $\frac{11}{8} \times \frac{8}{9}$ is _____ $\frac{11}{8}$.

9 Select all the fractions that would result in a product that is less than 1,254.

$$\blacksquare \times 1,254$$

Ⓐ $\frac{17}{18}$

Ⓑ $\frac{18}{17}$

Ⓒ $\frac{16}{16}$

Ⓓ $\frac{16}{17}$

Ⓔ $\frac{17}{17}$

Spiral Review

10 Estimate the difference.

$9\frac{7}{10} - 3\frac{1}{5}$

11 Write the expression using a common denominator.

$2\frac{2}{5} + 3\frac{2}{10}$

Multiply Fractions

1 Prices in the year 2000 were about $\frac{4}{5}$ what they are today. About how much more does a $25,000 vehicle cost today than the same vehicle cost in 2000?

_____

2 The population of Bactrian camels in Mongolia is about $\frac{7}{12}$ of the population of Bactrian camels in China. The estimated number of Bactrian camels in China is shown. About how many Bactrian camels are in Mongolia? Write an equation to model the problem.

Population: 600

_____

_____

Find the product.

3 $\frac{6}{7} \times 12$ _____

4 $\frac{5}{6} \times \frac{7}{8}$ _____

5 $\frac{7}{12} \times \frac{4}{5}$ _____

6 (MP) **Construct Arguments** Mr. Gupta makes wooden dolls by hand. A toy store asks if he can send them 63 dolls. Mr Gupta offers two options to the store.

- He can send the store $\frac{7}{9}$ of this amount by the end of the week.
- He can send the store 9 dolls a week for the next 7 weeks.

How many fewer dolls will the store receive if they select the first option? Why might the store prefer the first option?

_____

7 **STEM** The owners of a nature preserve calculate the amount of land needed to support a community of 150 zebra and 40 antelope. In order to provide enough grass and plants necessary for food, 2 acres of land are needed for each zebra and $\frac{1}{2}$ acre of land is needed for each antelope. How many acres of land are needed to support all the animals?

_____

Test Prep

8 Which fraction of 960 is equal to 720?

(A) $\frac{4}{6}$

(C) $\frac{3}{5}$

(B) $\frac{3}{4}$

(D) $\frac{4}{3}$

9 The original price of a computer is $1,200. The computer is on sale at four stores. Ben's Warehouse sells the computer for $\frac{3}{4}$ of the original price. Carl's Computers sells it for $\frac{2}{3}$ of the original price. Deidra's Technology sells it for $\frac{7}{8}$ of the original price, and Ellen's Electronics sells it for $\frac{5}{6}$ of the original price. Draw lines to match each store with the sale price.

Ben's Warehouse •   • $800

Carl's Computers •   • $900

Deidra's Technology •   • $1,000

Ellen's Electronics •   • $1,050

10 The resale value of a brand new vehicle that costs $18,900 decreases by $4,200 once it is driven 10,000 miles.

Write *equal to*, *greater than*, or *less than*.

This decrease is _____ $\frac{2}{9}$ of the vehicle's cost.

11 More than half of all primate species are at risk for extinction. There are approximately 500 primate species. What is a possible fraction of these primate species that are at risk for extinction? How many are at risk based on your fraction?

_____

Spiral Review

12 Use a visual model to solve.

$\frac{2}{3}$ of 36 _____

13 Estimate the difference.

$$3\frac{1}{10} - 1\frac{2}{3}$$

Estimate: _____

LESSON 9.1
**More Practice/
Homework**

ONLINE
Video Tutorials and
Interactive Examples

Explore Area and Mixed Numbers

1 (MP) **Use Tools** Marisol hangs a painting on the wall. What is the area of the painting? Use the rectangle to draw an area model. Then solve the problem.

$1\frac{1}{3}$ ft

$2\frac{1}{4}$ ft

_____

Use the rectangle to draw an area model to find the product.

2 $4\frac{2}{3} \times 1\frac{1}{2}$

3 $2\frac{1}{2} \times 3\frac{1}{2}$

_____

_____

4 **Math on the Spot** Terrence is designing a garden. He drew this diagram of his garden. Pose a problem using mixed numbers that can be solved using his diagram. Then solve the problem.

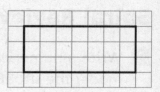

_____

_____

_____

Test Prep

5 Which product could be represented by the shaded part of the area model?

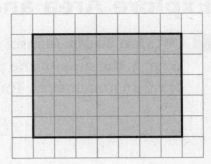

Ⓐ $2\frac{1}{2} \times 2\frac{1}{3}$ Ⓒ $1\frac{2}{3} \times 2\frac{1}{3}$

Ⓑ $1\frac{1}{4} \times 2\frac{1}{4}$ Ⓓ $2\frac{1}{2} \times 1\frac{3}{4}$

6 A rectangular-shaped mural has a length of $1\frac{2}{3}$ feet and a width of $1\frac{1}{4}$ feet. Which is the area of the mural?

Ⓐ $1\frac{1}{12}$ sq ft Ⓑ $1\frac{2}{12}$ sq ft Ⓒ $2\frac{1}{12}$ sq ft Ⓓ $2\frac{2}{12}$ sq ft

7 Select all the products equivalent to $3\frac{3}{4}$.

Ⓐ $2\frac{1}{2} \times 1\frac{1}{2}$

Ⓑ $1\frac{1}{2} \times 2\frac{1}{6}$

Ⓒ $2\frac{1}{4} \times 1\frac{2}{3}$

Ⓓ $1\frac{1}{8} \times 3\frac{1}{3}$

Ⓔ $1\frac{1}{4} \times 2\frac{3}{5}$

8 The diagram shows the dimensions of a rectangular wall. What is the area of the wall?

_____

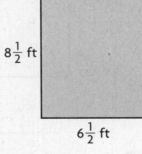

$8\frac{1}{2}$ ft

$6\frac{1}{2}$ ft

Spiral Review

9 Write a numerical expression to model the situation.

Carson buys 3 bags of pretzels at $2 each.

_____

10 Jamie takes $\frac{1}{4}$-yard strips of ribbon and cuts them into pieces that are $\frac{1}{3}$ the length. How long are the resulting pieces of ribbon?

_____

LESSON 9.2
**More Practice/
Homework**

ONLINE
Video Tutorials and
Interactive Examples

Multiply Mixed Numbers

1 Health and Fitness Trail running is an exercise that involves running on trails instead of paved roads to reduce the impact on ankles and knees. Samantha runs on the Lakeside Trail. She runs $2\frac{1}{2}$ times around the loop and then walks the remainder of the way. How far does Samantha run? Write an equation to model the distance Samantha runs.

Lakeside Trail
$2\frac{1}{4}$-mile loop

_____

2 (MP) **Use Tools** Jeeran is making a rectangular banner for school. The dimensions of the banner are $1\frac{1}{2}$ yards by $1\frac{3}{4}$ yards. What is the area of the banner?

Use the visual model to show the area. Then write an equation to model the problem.

_____

Multiply.

3 $1\frac{3}{5} \times 2\frac{1}{2}$

4 $4\frac{2}{3} \times 2\frac{2}{3}$

5 $3\frac{5}{8} \times 1\frac{1}{2}$

_____

6 $2\frac{1}{3} \times 2\frac{3}{4}$

7 $3\frac{1}{5} \times 1\frac{2}{3}$

8 $5\frac{1}{2} \times 3\frac{3}{4}$

_____

9 (MP) **Model with Mathematics** Jonathan uses this area model to show the product of two mixed numbers. What equation models the product?

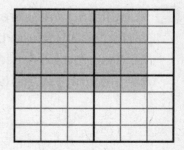

_____

10 Math on the Spot Cara's muffin recipe calls for $1\frac{1}{2}$ cups of flour for the muffins and $\frac{1}{4}$ cup of flour for the topping. If she makes $\frac{1}{2}$ of the original recipe, how much flour will she use?

Test Prep

11 Which mixed number is equivalent to $3\frac{1}{6} \times 2\frac{1}{2}$?

   Ⓐ $5\frac{1}{4}$ Ⓒ $7\frac{1}{2}$

   Ⓑ $6\frac{1}{12}$ Ⓓ $7\frac{11}{12}$

12 Nandani has 6 cups of flour. Her muffin recipe calls for $1\frac{1}{2}$ cups of flour for one batch of muffins. How much flour does she have left after making $1\frac{1}{2}$ batches of muffins?

   Ⓐ $3\frac{3}{4}$ cups   Ⓒ $2\frac{1}{2}$ cups

   Ⓑ 3 cups   Ⓓ $2\frac{1}{4}$ cups

13 Each day, Jarrod walks $1\frac{3}{4}$ miles to school and back home. Isaiah walks $1\frac{1}{3}$ times as far as Jarrod walks. How many miles does Isaiah walk to school and back home each day? Write an equation to model the problem.

_____

14 Cynthia is using tiles that measure $\frac{1}{2}$ foot by $\frac{1}{2}$ foot to tile a rectangular countertop that measures $8\frac{1}{2}$ feet by $3\frac{1}{2}$ feet. How many tiles will she use?

_____

Spiral Review

15 A building measures 45 feet tall. The building is rescaled as modeled by the expressions shown. Use *shorter*, *taller*, or *same* to describe how the height of the rescaled building compares to the original height.

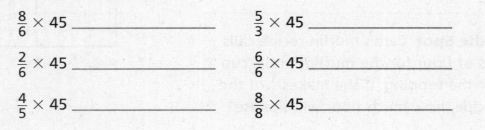

   $\frac{8}{6} \times 45$ _____ $\frac{5}{3} \times 45$ _____

   $\frac{2}{6} \times 45$ _____ $\frac{6}{6} \times 45$ _____

   $\frac{4}{5} \times 45$ _____ $\frac{8}{8} \times 45$ _____

LESSON 9.3
**More Practice/
Homework**

ONLINE
Video Tutorials and
Interactive Examples

Practice Multiplication with Fractions and Mixed Numbers

1 (MP) **Model with Mathematics** A mattress measures $6\frac{1}{4}$ feet by $3\frac{1}{4}$ feet.

• What is the area of the top of the mattress? Write an equation using fractions greater than 1 to model the problem.

_____

• Rewrite the area of the mattress using a mixed number.

_____

• The top of a second mattress has $1\frac{1}{2}$ times as much area as the first mattress. What is the area of the top of the second mattress? Write an equation to model the problem.

_____

2 (MP) **Model with Mathematics** A pet shop has 4 fish tanks. Each tank holds $8\frac{3}{4}$ gallons. How many gallons do the 4 fish tanks hold? Write an equation to model the problem.

_____

Find the product.

3 $3 \times 2\frac{3}{7}$

4 $\frac{4}{5} \times 1\frac{3}{4}$

5 $2\frac{3}{8} \times 4\frac{1}{2}$

_____ _____ _____

6 $4\frac{3}{8} \times 1\frac{1}{2}$

7 $7\frac{3}{9} \times 5$

8 $6\frac{3}{5} \times \frac{3}{4}$

_____ _____ _____

9 (MP) **Critique Reasoning** Akifumi says that he can find $1\frac{1}{2}$ times as much as 20 by finding the quotient of 20 and 2, and then adding 20, for a total of 30. Is he correct? Why or why not?

_____

_____

_____

Test Prep

10 A rectangular sports court measures $5\frac{1}{2}$ yards by $7\frac{3}{4}$ yards. Which is the area of the sports court?

Ⓐ $42\frac{5}{8}$ sq yd

Ⓑ $35\frac{3}{8}$ sq yd

Ⓒ $28\frac{5}{8}$ sq yd

Ⓓ $12\frac{2}{3}$ sq yd

11 Lonny is checking how close the bus stops are to where he is standing. One bus stop is $\frac{2}{5}$ mile away. A second bus stop is 3 times as far away. How far from where Lonny is standing is the second bus stop?

Ⓐ $3\frac{2}{5}$ miles

Ⓑ 3 miles

Ⓒ $1\frac{1}{5}$ miles

Ⓓ $\frac{5}{6}$ mile

12 Which mixed number is equivalent to $4 \times 3\frac{3}{5}$?

Ⓐ $12\frac{1}{5}$

Ⓑ $12\frac{3}{5}$

Ⓒ $14\frac{2}{5}$

Ⓓ $14\frac{3}{5}$

13 Halim has $3\frac{3}{4}$ gallons of paint. He determines that he needs 3 times as much as that amount for a project he is doing. How much paint does he need? Write an equation to model the problem.

_____

14 While training for a 10-kilometer race, Tracy ran $8\frac{2}{3}$ miles in 3 days. Her twin sister Tamara ran $1\frac{1}{2}$ times as much as Tracy in the same 3 days. How many miles did Tamara run in 3 days? Write an equation to model the problem.

_____

Spiral Review

15 Compare the numerical expressions.

$(23 + 47)$ and $3 \times (23 + 47)$

16 Use parentheses to rewrite the numerical expression so that it has a value of 18.

$2 + 4 \times 7 - 3$

_____

Name _____

LESSON 9.4
**More Practice/
Homework**

ONLINE
Video Tutorials and
Interactive Examples

Apply Fraction Multiplication to Find Area

1 Hal is painting a wall that measures $10\frac{1}{4}$ feet by 9 feet. What is the area of the wall?

_____

2 (MP) **Model with Mathematics** A rug is $2\frac{3}{5}$ feet wide and 6 feet long. What is the area of the rug? Write an equation to model the problem.

_____

Find the area of the rectangle.

3

$5\frac{1}{4}$ ft

$2\frac{3}{5}$ ft

_____

4

$3\frac{3}{4}$ in.

$2\frac{2}{3}$ in.

_____

5

3 yd

$2\frac{7}{8}$ yd

_____

6

$\frac{3}{4}$ mi

$\frac{2}{3}$ mi

_____

7 (MP) **Attend to Precision** Caleb needs to place a ground cover under a tent. The floor of the tent measures $8\frac{3}{4}$ feet by $9\frac{2}{3}$ feet. He purchases a ground cover that states that it covers 90 square feet. Will the ground cover be able to be used under the tent? Explain your reasoning.

_____

_____

_____

_____

Test Prep

8 Which is the area of the rectangle?

- (A) $24\frac{15}{16}$ sq ft
- (B) $20\frac{3}{16}$ sq ft
- (C) $20\frac{1}{16}$ sq ft
- (D) $12\frac{2}{5}$ sq ft

$2\frac{3}{8}$ ft $\boxed{}$ $10\frac{1}{2}$ ft

9 Select all the sets of dimensions of a rectangle with an area greater than 8 square inches.

- (A) $3\frac{1}{2}$ inches by $2\frac{3}{5}$ inches
- (B) 4 inches by $1\frac{2}{5}$ inches
- (C) 5 inches by $1\frac{3}{4}$ inches
- (D) 10 inches by $\frac{3}{4}$ inches
- (E) $2\frac{2}{3}$ inches by $3\frac{1}{5}$ inches

10 Uyen measures two rectangular tabletops. The green tabletop has dimensions of 7 feet by $4\frac{1}{2}$ feet. The area of the brown tabletop is $1\frac{1}{2}$ times as great as the area of the green tabletop. What is the area of the brown tabletop?

_____

11 Mr. King is placing tile on the entry hall of a museum. The entry hall is rectangular with dimensions of $20\frac{3}{4}$ feet by 15 feet. What is the area of the entry hall?

_____

Spiral Review

12 Use fraction strips to find the difference. Draw to show your thinking.

$\frac{7}{6} - \frac{1}{3} =$ _____

13 Multiply.

$3\frac{1}{6} \times 2\frac{2}{5} =$ _____

LESSON 10.1
**More Practice/
Homework**

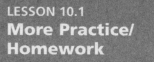

 **ONLINE**
Video Tutorials and
Interactive Examples

Interpret a Fraction as Division

1 **Geography** The United States can be divided into
5 geographical regions: Northeast, Southwest, West,
Southeast, and Midwest. A teacher plans 3 hours to
discuss the 5 regions equally. For how many hours
will the class discuss each region? Draw a visual model
to represent the situation and find the quotient.

_____

(MP) Model with Mathematics Model the situation with a
division equation and find the quotient.

2 Sanjay, Margo, and Deidre
share 2 jars of paint equally.
How many jars of paint does
each receive?

3 A pizza is cut into 10 equal slices.
Eight friends each eat 1 slice.
How much of the pizza did the
friends eat?

_____ _____

4 **(MP) Attend to Precision** Two groups of friends are sharing
apples of the same size. The first group of 3 friends share
4 apples. The second group of 4 friends share 6 apples. All of
the friends share their apples equally. Which group of friends
gets a greater portion of apple? Explain.

_____

_____

_____

5 **Math on the Spot** Eight students share 12 mini oatmeal muffins
equally and 6 students share 15 mini apple muffins equally.
Carmine is in both groups of students. What is the total number
of mini muffins Carmine gets?

_____

Test Prep

6 Which expression is equivalent to $\frac{7}{18}$?

(A) $18 - 7$

(B) 7×18

(C) $7 \div 18$

(D) $18 \div 7$

7 Maria cans 6 quarts of tomato sauce. She divides the tomato sauce equally into 8 jars. How much of a quart of tomato sauce is in each jar? Model the situation with a division equation and find the quotient.

_____

8 Kiara has a bag with 9 oranges. She shares the oranges between 3 friends and herself. Write an equation to model the situation. How many oranges does each person receive?

_____

9 Mr. Thomas has a board that is 5 feet long. He wants each of his 6 students to have an equal-sized piece of the board for carving their names. What should be the length of each piece of the board? Represent the situation with an equation or visual model and solve.

_____

Spiral Review

10 Find the product.

$\frac{5}{9} \times 63$

11 Use the visual model to find the product.

$2 \times \frac{4}{6}$

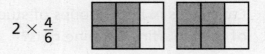

Name _____

Represent and Find the Size of Equal Parts

1 (MP) **Use Tools** A pitcher contains $\frac{1}{2}$ gallon of lemonade. Emma needs to pour an equal amount of lemonade into each of 2 smaller pitchers.

- Draw a visual model to represent $\frac{1}{2} \div 2$.

- What is the quotient? _____

- Write a division equation that includes your quotient to model this situation. Explain what the quotient represents.

_____

_____

Divide.

2 $\frac{1}{5} \div 2$

_____

3 $\frac{1}{3} \div 4$

_____

4 $\frac{1}{8} \div 4$

_____

5 $\frac{1}{10} \div 4$

_____

6 $\frac{1}{4} \div 2$

_____

7 $\frac{1}{6} \div 4$

_____

8 Landon is painting a mural. His plan is to paint $\frac{1}{5}$ of the mural over 5 days, painting equal sections each day. How much of the mural will Landon paint each day?

_____

9 (MP) **Construct Arguments** Scott has $\frac{1}{2}$ yard of string to make friendship bracelets. Each bracelet requires $\frac{1}{4}$ yard of string. Can Scott make 4 friendship bracelets with the string he has? Explain.

_____

_____

Test Prep

10 Olivia has $\frac{1}{8}$ pound of butter. She needs to divide the butter equally among 4 batches of muffins she is baking. How much butter is used in each batch of muffins?

    Ⓐ $\frac{1}{32}$ pound   Ⓒ 2 pounds

    Ⓑ $\frac{1}{12}$ pound   Ⓓ 4 pounds

11 DeSean and 6 of his friends are carrying $\frac{1}{5}$ of a load of wood equally. How much of the load does each person carry?

    Ⓐ $\frac{1}{35}$ Ⓒ $\frac{1}{12}$

    Ⓑ $\frac{1}{30}$ Ⓓ $\frac{1}{11}$

12 Divide. $\frac{1}{12} \div 4$

_____

13 Kelly can run $\frac{1}{2}$ mile in 3 minutes. How far does Kelly run in 1 minute if he runs at the same pace the entire time?

_____

14 A farmer orders $\frac{1}{5}$ ton of hay for the horses and the cows. If the horses and the cows are each given the same amount, how much hay are the horses and the cows each given?

_____

Spiral Review

15 Jenny uses half of a garden space to plant roses. She uses $\frac{1}{4}$ of that space to plant pink roses. What fraction of the entire space does Jenny use for pink roses?

_____

16 Divide.

    $316 \div 23$

_____

© Houghton Mifflin Harcourt Publishing Company

Name _____

LESSON 10.3
More Practice/ Homework

ONLINE
Video Tutorials and
Interactive Examples

Use Representations of Division of Unit Fractions by Whole Numbers

1 (MP) **Critique Reasoning** The load of dirt is going to be divided into 10 containers. Raj says each container will have 5 tons of dirt.

$\frac{1}{2}$ **ton of dirt**

- What error did Raj make?

_____

_____

- What is the correct amount of dirt in each container?

_____

(MP) **Model with Mathematics** Write a word problem that can be modeled by the expression. Then draw a visual model and solve your problem.

2 $\frac{1}{4} \div 6$

3 $\frac{1}{6} \div 5$

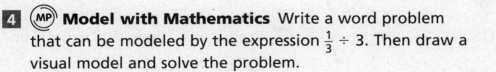

4 (MP) **Model with Mathematics** Write a word problem that can be modeled by the expression $\frac{1}{3} \div 3$. Then draw a visual model and solve the problem.

_____

_____

Test Prep

5 Which expression could represent the visual model?

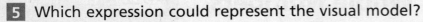

- (A) $3 \div 4$
- (B) $4 \div \frac{1}{3}$
- (C) $\frac{1}{4} \div 3$
- (D) $3 \div \frac{1}{4}$

6 Write a division equation to represent the visual model.

_____

7 Write a word problem that can be represented by the expression $\frac{1}{5} \div 4$. Then draw a visual model and solve your problem.

_____

_____

_____

Spiral Review

8 Find the product.

$$\frac{2}{3} \times \frac{3}{4}$$

9 Evaluate the numerical expression.

$$(9 - 2) \times (3 + 7)$$

_____

Represent and Find the Number of Equal-Sized Parts

1 (MP) **Model with Mathematics** The visual model represents $3 \div \frac{1}{6}$. Write a division equation that represents the visual model.

1	1	1
$\frac{1}{6}$ $\frac{1}{6}$ $\frac{1}{6}$ $\frac{1}{6}$ $\frac{1}{6}$ $\frac{1}{6}$	$\frac{1}{6}$ $\frac{1}{6}$ $\frac{1}{6}$ $\frac{1}{6}$ $\frac{1}{6}$ $\frac{1}{6}$	$\frac{1}{6}$ $\frac{1}{6}$ $\frac{1}{6}$ $\frac{1}{6}$ $\frac{1}{6}$ $\frac{1}{6}$

_____

(MP) **Use Tools** Draw a visual model to represent the expression. Then find the quotient.

2 $2 \div \frac{1}{5}$ _____

3 $4 \div \frac{1}{4}$ _____

4 **STEM** Earth and Mars orbit the Sun. Each time Earth makes one complete orbit, Mars makes about $\frac{1}{2}$ of its orbit. How many orbits does Earth make around the Sun in the time it takes Mars to complete 6 orbits?

_____

5 (MP) **Model with Mathematics** Kat uses $\frac{1}{2}$ gallon of water each day on a camping trip. Her water jug holds 5 gallons of water. How many days will Kat have water to use if she fills her water jug completely before leaving? Draw a visual model to solve the problem. Write a division equation to model the problem.

_____

Test Prep

6 Darren has 10 pounds of carrots. He divides the carrots into $\frac{1}{2}$-pound bags. How many bags of carrots does Darren make?

(A) 5   (B) 8   (C) 12   (D) 20

7 Select all the division expressions that have a quotient of 24.

(A) $4 \div \frac{1}{6}$ (D) $\frac{1}{6} \div 4$

(B) $6 \div \frac{1}{4}$ (E) $8 \div \frac{1}{3}$

(C) $\frac{1}{4} \div 6$ (F) $\frac{1}{3} \div 8$

8 Write an equation that represents the visual model.

Number line from 0 to 3 marked in fifths: 0, $\frac{1}{5}$, $\frac{2}{5}$, $\frac{3}{5}$, $\frac{4}{5}$, 1, $1\frac{1}{5}$, $1\frac{2}{5}$, $1\frac{3}{5}$, $1\frac{4}{5}$, 2, $2\frac{1}{5}$, $2\frac{2}{5}$, $2\frac{3}{5}$, $2\frac{4}{5}$, 3

_____

9 An 8-mile running path is divided into $\frac{1}{4}$-mile sections for running sprints. How many sections for running sprints does the path have? Draw a visual model to solve the problem.

_____

Spiral Review

10 Draw a visual model to find $\frac{3}{5} \times \frac{2}{3}$.   **11** Find the product $\frac{2}{5} \times \frac{5}{8}$.

LESSON 10.5
**More Practice/
Homework**

 ONLINE
Video Tutorials and
Interactive Examples

Use Representations of Division of Whole Numbers by Unit Fractions

1 **Open Ended** Gabe uses the expression $7 \div \frac{1}{3}$ to solve a problem.

- Write a word problem that can be modeled by the expression.

_____

_____

- Draw a visual model to represent the word problem and find the quotient.

_____

2 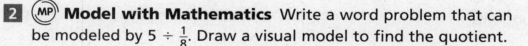 **Model with Mathematics** Write a word problem that can be modeled by $5 \div \frac{1}{8}$. Draw a visual model to find the quotient.

_____

_____

Find the quotient.

3 $8 \div \frac{1}{4}$

_____

4 $9 \div \frac{1}{5}$

_____

5 $3 \div \frac{1}{7}$

_____

6 $6 \div \frac{1}{6}$

_____

7 $4 \div \frac{1}{3}$

_____

8 $5 \div \frac{1}{2}$

_____

Test Prep

9 Write and solve a word problem about pizza that can be modeled by the expression $6 \div \frac{1}{8}$. Draw a visual model to find the quotient.

_____

_____

10 Write and solve a word problem that can be modeled by the expression $4 \div \frac{1}{5}$. Draw a visual model to find the quotient.

_____

_____

11 Find the quotient.

$10 \div \frac{1}{10}$ _____

12 Ashlyn is making jump ropes from a coil of rope. A jump rope is $\frac{1}{4}$ of the coil. How many jump ropes can Ashlyn make from 7 coils of rope? Draw a visual model and solve.

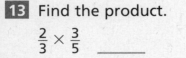

Spiral Review

13 Find the product.

$\frac{2}{3} \times \frac{3}{5}$ _____

$2 \times \frac{3}{12}$ _____

14 Estimate. Then find the difference.

$6\frac{1}{8} - 4\frac{3}{10}$

_____

LESSON 11.1
**More Practice/
Homework**

ONLINE
Video Tutorials and
Interactive Examples

Relate Multiplication and Division of Fractions

(MP) **Model with Mathematics** Represent the situation with a visual model. Then write a division equation and a related multiplication equation.

1 Marcos has 4 gallons of gasoline for a lawn mower. How many lawns can he mow if each lawn uses $\frac{1}{4}$ gallon of gasoline?

2 Mrs. Sorel has $\frac{1}{2}$ ton of topsoil delivered to use in 5 gardens. If each garden gets the same amount, how much topsoil does each garden get?

_____

_____

_____

_____

Divide. Write a related multiplication equation to solve.

3 $7 \div \frac{1}{5} = x$

4 $x = 9 \div \frac{1}{9}$

5 $\frac{1}{6} \div 5 = x$

_____

_____

_____

6 $3 \div \frac{1}{10} = x$

7 $x = \frac{1}{8} \div 2$

8 $x = \frac{1}{2} \div 10$

_____

_____

_____

9 **Math on the Spot** The slowest mammal is the three-toed sloth. The top speed of a three-toed sloth on the ground is about $\frac{1}{4}$ foot per second. The top speed of a giant tortoise on the ground is about $\frac{1}{3}$ foot per second. How much longer would it take a three-toed sloth than a giant tortoise to travel 12 feet on the ground?

_____

Test Prep

10 Jorge drew a visual model to represent dividing a whole number by a unit fraction. Which equation represents the visual model?

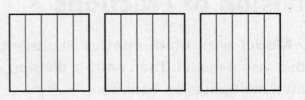

Ⓐ $3 \div \frac{1}{15} = 45$

Ⓑ $15 \div \frac{1}{3} = 45$

Ⓒ $3 \div \frac{1}{5} = 15$

Ⓓ $15 \div \frac{1}{5} = 75$

11 Select all the quotients that are greater than 1.

Ⓐ $1 \div \frac{1}{3}$

Ⓑ $\frac{1}{4} \div 3$

Ⓒ $\frac{1}{5} \div 7$

Ⓓ $5 \div \frac{1}{10}$

Ⓔ $2 \div \frac{1}{2}$

12 There is $\frac{1}{5}$ of a cartridge of color printer ink left in a printer. The printer program shows that this is enough to print 4 more color photographs. If each photograph uses the same amount of ink, how much of a cartridge is used for each photograph?

Spiral Review

13 Five students in a class take turns speaking during a 6-minute presentation. If each student speaks for an equal amount of time, how long does each student speak?

14 Find the product.

$4 \times 1\frac{3}{4}$

Name _____

LESSON 11.2
More Practice/ Homework

ONLINE
Video Tutorials and
Interactive Examples

Divide Whole Numbers by Unit Fractions

1 (MP) **Model with Mathematics** A hiking trail has a marker every $\frac{1}{4}$ mile. How many markers are on the trail? Write a division equation to model the situation. Then write a related multiplication equation to solve.

Mountain Cabin Trail 8 miles

_____

2 Jesse uses about $\frac{1}{3}$ pound of chalk for each gymnastics tournament he attends. For how many tournaments will 7 pounds of chalk last? Write a division equation to model the situation. Then write a related multiplication equation to solve.

_____

_____

Divide. Write a related multiplication equation to solve.

3 $9 \div \frac{1}{5} = n$ **4** $n = 3 \div \frac{1}{8}$ **5** $n = 2 \div \frac{1}{12}$

_____   _____   _____

6 (MP) **Use Structure** Jessica uses a number line to represent the division of a whole number by a unit fraction.

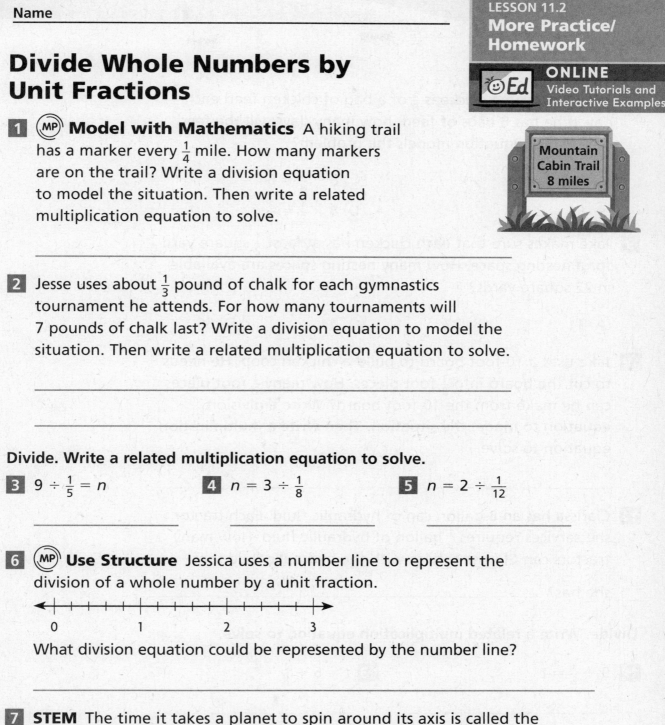

What division equation could be represented by the number line?

_____

7 **STEM** The time it takes a planet to spin around its axis is called the rotation period. It takes about 1 day for Earth to complete a rotation. Each time Earth completes one rotation, Saturn completes about $\frac{1}{2}$ of its rotation. How many rotations has Earth made in 15 Saturn days? Write a division equation to model the situation. Then write a related multiplication equation to solve.

_____

_____

Test Prep

8 Jake feeds some chickens $\frac{1}{8}$ of a bag of chicken feed each day. If he has 8 bags of feed, how many days will the feed last? Which equation models the problem?

Ⓐ $\frac{1}{8} \div 8 = \frac{1}{64}$

Ⓒ $8 \div \frac{1}{8} = 64$

Ⓑ $64 \div 8 = 8$

Ⓓ $8 \times \frac{1}{8} = \frac{8}{8}$

9 Jake makes sure that each chicken has at least $\frac{1}{2}$ square yard for a nesting space. How many nesting spaces are available in 22 square yards?

Ⓐ 11   Ⓑ 22   Ⓒ 44   Ⓓ 66

10 Jake uses a 10-foot board to build a chicken coop. He needs to cut the board into $\frac{1}{2}$ foot pieces. How many $\frac{1}{2}$ foot pieces can he make from the 10-foot board? Write a division equation to model the situation. Then write a multiplication equation to solve.

_____

11 Clarissa has an 8-gallon can of hydraulic fluid. Each tractor she services requires $\frac{1}{3}$ gallon of hydraulic fluid. How many tractors can Clarissa service with the hydraulic fluid that

she has? _____

Divide. Write a related multiplication equation to solve.

12 $9 \div \frac{1}{5} = t$

_____

13 $t = 6 \div \frac{1}{8}$

_____

Spiral Review

14 Divide.

$\frac{1}{6} \div 3 =$ _____

$\frac{1}{8} \div 4 =$ _____

15 Find the product.

$2\frac{1}{2} \times 2\frac{2}{3}$

_____

LESSON 11.3
**More Practice/
Homework**

ONLINE
Video Tutorials and
Interactive Examples

Interpret and Solve Division of a Whole Number by a Unit Fraction

1 (MP) **Use Tools** Write and solve a division word problem for the visual model.

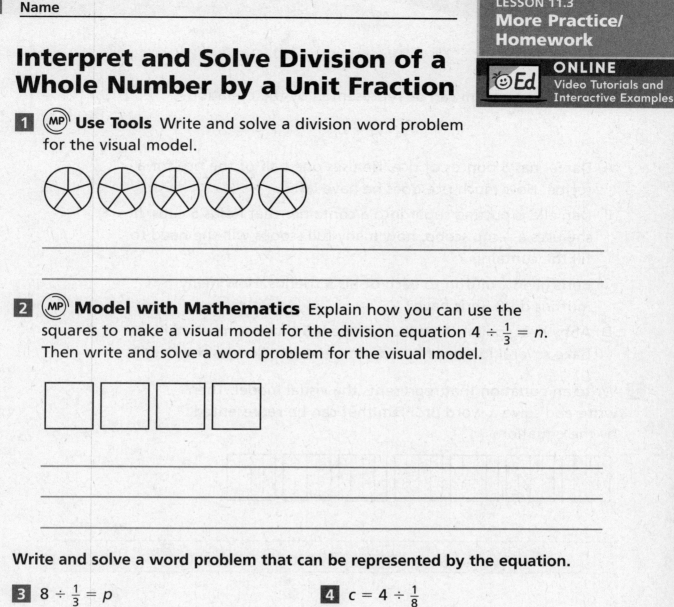

_____

_____

2 (MP) **Model with Mathematics** Explain how you can use the squares to make a visual model for the division equation $4 \div \frac{1}{3} = n$. Then write and solve a word problem for the visual model.

_____

_____

_____

Write and solve a word problem that can be represented by the equation.

3 $8 \div \frac{1}{3} = p$

_____

_____

_____

4 $c = 4 \div \frac{1}{8}$

_____

_____

_____

5 (MP) **Use Tools** Write a word problem that can be modeled by the equation $s = 5 \div \frac{1}{4}$. Draw a visual model to represent the equation. Then solve.

_____

_____

_____

Test Prep

6 Which word problem can be represented by the equation?

$$5 \div \frac{1}{2} = n$$

  Ⓐ Daniel has 5 ounces of rice. He uses one half of the rice for a recipe. How much rice does he have left?

  Ⓑ Danielle is putting sugar into a container that holds 5 cups. If she uses a $\frac{1}{2}$-cup scoop, how many full scoops will she need to fill the container?

  Ⓒ Boris gives $\frac{1}{2}$ muffin to each of his 5 friends. How many muffins does Boris have?

  Ⓓ Abby has $\frac{1}{2}$ gallon of milk. She needs 5 times as much milk to bake several loaves of bread. How much milk does she need?

7 Write an equation that represents the visual model. Then write and solve a word problem that can be represented by the equation.

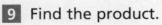

_____

_____

Spiral Review

8 Joanie has $\frac{1}{4}$ hour left in her day at work. She has 3 shelves to restock. If she spends an equal amount of time on each shelf, how long will it take her to restock one shelf? Draw a visual model to represent the problem and solve.

_____

9 Find the product.

$4\frac{2}{3} \times \frac{3}{4}$ _____

$2\frac{5}{6} \times 1\frac{1}{3}$ _____

Name _____

LESSON 11.4
More Practice/ Homework

ONLINE
Video Tutorials and
Interactive Examples

Divide Unit Fractions by Whole Numbers

1 **Social Studies** Citizens in the United States must register to vote for local, state, and national elections. Farris helps with voter registration. He delivers $\frac{1}{2}$ box of registration forms equally to 3 voter sites. What fraction of the box does Farris deliver to each site? Draw a visual model and write an equation to represent the problem.

2 (MP) **Use Tools** Cal orders $\frac{1}{4}$ ton of gravel to use in 2 cactus beds. If he uses the same amount in each bed, how much gravel does he use in one bed? Write an equation to model the situation. Then represent the problem on the number line.

0   1

Divide. Write a related multiplication equation to solve.

3 $\frac{1}{3} \div 3 = n$

4 $n = \frac{1}{7} \div 5$

5 $\frac{1}{9} \div 2 = n$

6 $\frac{1}{6} \div 8 = n$

7 $n = \frac{1}{2} \div 7$

8 $n = \frac{1}{8} \div 9$

9 (MP) **Reason** Devin has $\frac{1}{2}$ pound of butter. He divides the butter into 2 equal parts. He then divides one of the parts into 5 equal parts to make butter pats for a dinner gathering. What fraction of a pound is one butter pat? Write two equations to model the problem.

Test Prep

10 Kelli has a wooden rod that is $\frac{1}{3}$ yard long. She cuts the rod into 4 equal-sized pieces. What is the size of each piece?

    (A) $\frac{3}{4}$ yd   (B) $\frac{1}{5}$ yd   (C) $\frac{1}{7}$ yd   (D) $\frac{1}{12}$ yd

11 Divide. Write a related multiplication equation to solve.

$\frac{1}{10} \div 5 = x$

_____

12 Wade has $\frac{1}{2}$ pound of silver. He makes 10 medallions from the silver. If he uses the same amount in each medallion, how much silver is used in one medallion? Represent the problem on the number line.

_____

13 Lani has $\frac{1}{5}$ kilogram of cheese. She slices the cheese into 2 equal pieces. What is the weight of one piece of cheese?

_____

Spiral Review

14 Max has a 4-pound bag of trail mix. He takes $\frac{1}{6}$ pound of trail mix to school for a snack each day. How many days will the bag last? Represent the situation with a visual model and then write a division equation to model the problem.

15 The pep rally committee has 12 students that regularly show up to meetings. By the time of the big game, the membership increases by $4\frac{2}{3}$ times as many students. How many students are members by the big game? Write an equation to model the situation.

Name _____

Interpret and Solve Division of a Unit Fraction by a Whole Number

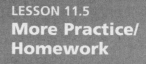

ONLINE
Video Tutorials and
Interactive Examples

1 **Use Tools** Write and solve a word problem that can be modeled by the equation $n = \frac{1}{4} \div 4$. Use the rectangle to draw a visual model to represent the quotient. Then interpret the quotient in the context of your story.

_____

_____

_____

_____

2 **Use Tools** Write a word problem that can be modeled by the equation $\frac{1}{2} \div 5 = x$. Draw a visual model to represent the quotient. Then interpret the quotient in the context of your problem.

_____

_____

_____

_____

Model with Mathematics Complete the word problem to represent the equation. Then write a related multiplication equation to solve.

3 $\frac{1}{2} \div 8 = p$

_____ pound of fish food is shared equally among _____ aquariums.

Each aquarium gets _____ pound of fish food.

_____

4 $g = \frac{1}{4} \div 5$

_____ gallon of paint is shared equally among _____ wooden toys.

Each toy is painted with _____ gallon of paint.

_____

Test Prep

5 Which word problem is modeled by the equation?

$$\frac{1}{4} \div 8 = n$$

(A) Doris uses $\frac{1}{4}$ cup of beads to make a bracelet. How many cups of beads will she need for 8 bracelets?

(B) Grant has 8 gallons of fuel in his car. This is enough fuel for $\frac{1}{4}$ of his trip. How many gallons will Grant need for his complete trip?

(C) Chris has $\frac{1}{4}$ pound of salt. He divides it equally among 8 salt shakers. How much salt does each shaker get?

(D) Geri has $\frac{1}{4}$ gallon of milk. She needs 8 times as much for a full week. How many gallons of milk does she need?

6 Write a word problem that can be modeled by the equation $\frac{1}{4} \div 2 = n$. Draw a visual model to represent the quotient. Then interpret the quotient in the context of your story.

_____

_____

_____

_____

Spiral Review

7 Find the quotient.

$5 \div \frac{1}{4} =$ _____

$6 \div \frac{1}{8} =$ _____

8 Use a visual model to solve.

$\frac{4}{5}$ of 40 _____

$\frac{2}{6}$ of 36 _____

LESSON 11.6
**More Practice/
Homework**

ONLINE
Video Tutorials and
Interactive Examples

Solve Division Problems Using Visual Models and Equations

1 (MP) **Use Tools** Mr. Jones needs 5 tons of gravel to pave a driveway at his farm. He can haul the gravel in $\frac{1}{5}$-ton loads in his small truck. How many loads will Mr. Jones need in order to haul all of the gravel? Draw a visual model to represent the situation and solve the problem. Then write a division equation to model the problem.

_____

2 (MP) **Model with Mathematics** Christie makes protein shakes for the swim team. She uses $\frac{1}{2}$ scoop of protein powder for each shake. How many shakes can Christie make if she has 6 full scoops of protein powder? Model the situation with a division equation and write a related multiplication equation to solve.

_____

_____

Divide. Write a related multiplication equation to solve.

3 $\frac{1}{4} \div 10 = r$ **4** $r = 11 \div \frac{1}{7}$ **5** $\frac{1}{9} \div 6 = r$

_____   _____   _____

6 (MP) **Model with Mathematics** A jewelry maker uses $\frac{1}{2}$ pound of silver to make 30 rings. If the same amount of silver is used for each ring, how much does one ring weigh? Model this situation with a division equation and write a related multiplication equation to solve.

_____

Test Prep

7 Mrs. Smith has $\frac{1}{2}$ gallon of orange juice. She divides it equally among her 8 grandchildren. How much orange juice does each grandchild get?

Which equation models the situation?

(A) $8 \times \frac{1}{2} = j$ (C) $\frac{1}{2} \div 8 = j$

(B) $2 \times 8 = j$ (D) $8 \div \frac{1}{2} = j$

8 Janis has 8 bags of fertilizer. She uses $\frac{1}{3}$ of a bag on each tree. How many trees can she fertilize with the 8 bags of fertilizer?

Which equation models the situation?

(A) $8 \times \frac{1}{3} = t$ (C) $\frac{1}{3} \div 8 = t$

(B) $8 \div \frac{1}{3} = t$ (D) $\frac{1}{8} \times \frac{1}{3} = t$

9 Henri has 9 equal-sized pieces of carpet. He uses $\frac{1}{2}$ piece of carpet to cover the floor of one doghouse. The floor of each doghouse is the same size. How many doghouse floors can the pieces of carpet cover? Draw a visual model to represent the situation and solve the problem. Then write a division equation to model the problem.

_____

10 What is the value of the expression $\frac{1}{8} \div 5$? _____

11 What is the value of the expression $6 \div \frac{1}{7}$? _____

Spiral Review

12 Use a visual model to find the product.

$\frac{2}{3} \times 24 =$ _____

$\frac{3}{8} \times 16 =$ _____

13 Draw a visual model to show $\frac{1}{4} \times \frac{1}{5}$.

Convert Customary Measurements

1 (MP) **Model with Mathematics** A mechanic has 160 fluid ounces of oil. She needs to put 1 quart of oil in each of 6 cars. Does she have enough oil? Write equations to solve the problem.

_____

_____

_____

Convert.

2 120 oz = _____ lb

3 19 qt = _____ gal

4 168 in. = _____ yd _____ ft

5 37 oz = _____ lb _____ oz

6 5 pt = _____ qt

7 440 yd = _____ mi

8 (MP) **Use Tools** The tape measure shows inches. Label the number of inches equivalent to $2\frac{1}{2}$, 3, $3\frac{1}{2}$, and 4 feet.

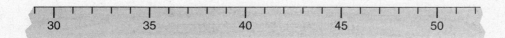

9 Kevin uses 48 ounces of dried apples and 22 ounces of dried cranberries to make a fruit snack. He plans to sell the snacks in $\frac{1}{2}$-pound containers. How many containers will he fill? Will any fruit snack be left over?

_____

_____

10 **STEM** Scientists have discovered a new glow-in-the-dark shark species that weighs up to 31 ounces when fully grown. About how much does an adult shark weigh in pounds?

_____

Test Prep

11 Lamar has 80 inches of ribbon to tie onto some balloons. He attaches 1 foot of ribbon to each balloon. How many balloons have ribbons?

_____

12 A store makes banners for a town parade. One banner is 1,224 inches long. The other banner is 2,196 inches long. Complete the table by finding the equivalent lengths in feet and yards.

Parade Banners		
Inches	Feet	Yards
1,224		
2,196		

13 Which measurements are greater than or equal to 56 fluid ounces? Select all that apply.

Ⓐ $\frac{1}{2}$ gallon

Ⓑ 2 quarts

Ⓒ $\frac{1}{4}$ gallon

Ⓓ $3\frac{1}{2}$ pints

Ⓔ 6 cups

Spiral Review

14 The veterinarian weighs two kittens. The striped kitten weighs $3\frac{1}{2}$ pounds. The gray kitten weighs $1\frac{3}{4}$ times as much as the striped kitten. How much does the gray kitten weigh?

_____

15 Joan and Wyatt are raking leaves. If Joan fills $3\frac{1}{6}$ bags and Wyatt fills $1\frac{1}{3}$ bags more than Joan, how many bags does Wyatt fill?

_____

Name _____

LESSON 12.2
More Practice/ Homework

ONLINE
Video Tutorials and
Interactive Examples

Solve Multistep Customary Measurement Problems

1 The first platform of the Eiffel Tower is 2,280 inches above the ground. The second platform is 376 feet above the ground. How many yards separate the first platform from the second platform?

_____

2 Henri buys 126 inches of a fabric that costs $12 for each yard. How much does Henri pay for the fabric?

_____

3 Elsa buys 27 quarts of punch for a party. Each serving is 8 fluid ounces. If the guests drink 100 servings of punch, how many fluid ounces of punch are left over?

_____

4 A truck travels 117 inches for each rotation of its tires. How many rotations do the tires make when the truck travels 5,200 yards?

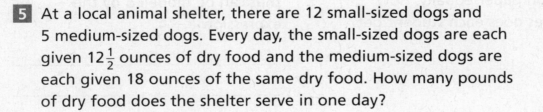

117 inches

_____

5 At a local animal shelter, there are 12 small-sized dogs and 5 medium-sized dogs. Every day, the small-sized dogs are each given $12\frac{1}{2}$ ounces of dry food and the medium-sized dogs are each given 18 ounces of the same dry food. How many pounds of dry food does the shelter serve in one day?

_____

Test Prep

6 Ms. Namgung's electric hedge trimmer has a 10-foot cord. Each of her extension cords is 50 feet long. The farthest hedge is 40 yards from the electrical outlet. How many extension cords will Ms. Namgung use to trim all the hedges? Explain.

_____

_____

_____

7 A recipe for stew calls for $2\frac{1}{2}$ pounds of meat, 22 ounces of beans, 14 ounces of carrots, and 2 pounds 6 ounces of potatoes. Which is the weight of the ingredients in the stew in pounds?

(A) $5\frac{1}{8}$ pounds

(B) $7\frac{1}{8}$ pounds

(C) 41 pounds

(D) 114 pounds

8 A crayon weighs $\frac{1}{2}$ ounce. There are 96 crayons in a box. The box weighs 4 ounces. How many pounds do 12 boxes of crayons weigh?

_____

Spiral Review

9 Three students share 10 pieces of construction paper equally. How many pieces does each student get?

10 Write and solve a word problem that can be modeled by the expression $\frac{1}{3} \div 4$.

_____

_____

_____

Name _____

Represent and Interpret Measurement Data in Line Plots

1 (MP) **Use Structure** Suraya records the heights of her classmates to the nearest $\frac{1}{8}$ inch. She makes a line plot of her data. Write a title for her line plot.

_____

Use the line plot for 2–5.

Lisa records the amounts of time she plans to spend for each reading session during a one-month period on the line plot.

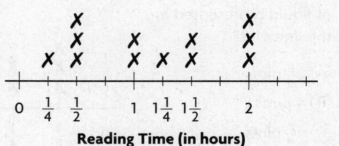

Reading Time (in hours)

2 How many reading sessions does Lisa plan to have during the month?

_____

3 How does the number of reading sessions longer than 1 hour compare to the number of sessions that are 1 hour or less?

_____

4 How much time will Lisa read during the one-month period?

_____

5 If Lisa redistributes the total time equally over all her reading sessions, how long will each session be?

_____

6 A breakfast chef used different amounts of milk when making pancakes, depending on the number of pancakes ordered. The results are shown below.

$\frac{1}{2}$ c, $\frac{1}{4}$ c, $\frac{1}{2}$ c, $\frac{3}{4}$ c, $\frac{1}{2}$ c, $\frac{3}{4}$ c, $\frac{1}{2}$ c, $\frac{1}{4}$ c, $\frac{1}{2}$ c, $\frac{1}{2}$ c

If the total milk used is equally redistributed among all the batches of pancakes, how much milk goes into each batch?

_____

Test Prep

7 Jeeran keeps track of the amounts of time for commercials during several one-hour programs. Complete the line plot to display the data.

$\frac{1}{4}$ hr, $\frac{1}{4}$ hr, $\frac{1}{8}$ hr, $\frac{1}{4}$ hr, $\frac{3}{8}$ hr, $\frac{3}{8}$ hr, $\frac{1}{4}$ hr

$\frac{1}{8}$ $\frac{1}{4}$ $\frac{3}{8}$

Commercial Time (in hours)

8 Which is the total amount of liquid represented in the line plot?

- (A) $2\frac{3}{4}$ pints
- (B) 4 pints
- (C) $4\frac{3}{8}$ pints
- (D) 11 pints

Liquid in Beakers (in pints)

0   $\frac{1}{8}$ $\frac{1}{4}$ $\frac{3}{8}$ $\frac{1}{2}$ $\frac{5}{8}$ $\frac{3}{4}$ $\frac{7}{8}$ 1

9 Zeb records the lengths of several insects. Select all the lengths that will be represented in a line plot using more than 2 *X*s.

$1\frac{1}{4}$ in., $1\frac{1}{8}$ in., $1\frac{3}{4}$ in., $1\frac{1}{2}$ in., $1\frac{3}{4}$ in., $1\frac{1}{4}$ in., $1\frac{1}{2}$ in., $2\frac{1}{4}$ in., $1\frac{3}{4}$ in., $1\frac{1}{2}$ in.

- (A) $1\frac{1}{8}$ in.
- (B) $1\frac{1}{4}$ in.
- (C) $1\frac{1}{2}$ in.
- (D) $1\frac{3}{4}$ in.
- (E) $2\frac{1}{4}$ in.

Spiral Review

10 Mr. Jonas's aquarium holds 8 gallons of water. If he buys another that holds $1\frac{1}{2}$ times as many gallons, how many gallons of water does Mr. Jonas's new tank hold?

11 Andie equally divides $\frac{1}{5}$ of a solution into 3 test tubes. How much of the solution is in each test tube?

Convert Time and Find Elapsed Time

1 Francine and her friends went on a hike along a mountain trail. How long were they on the hike? Write the amount of time in hours and then in minutes.

_____

9:15 a.m.   1:30 p.m.

START   FINISH

Convert.

2 525 sec = _____ min _____ sec

3 285 hr = _____ d _____ hr

4 117 wk = about _____ yr

5 450 min = _____ hr

Find the start, elapsed, or end time.

6 Start time: 7:30 a.m.

Elapsed time: $6\frac{1}{3}$ hr

End time: _____

7 Start time: 11:15 a.m.

Elapsed time: _____ hr

End time: 4:30 p.m.

Compare. Write <, >, or =.

8 7 wk $\bigcirc$ 44 d

9 4,800 sec $\bigcirc$ $1\frac{1}{2}$ hr

10 **Math on the Spot** Use the graph. Which service took the longest to download the podcast? How much longer did it take than Red Fox in minutes and seconds?

_____

_____

Podcast Download Time

Internet Service	Time (in seconds)
Top Hat	1,050
Groove Box	173
Jackrabbit	980
Internet-C	196
Red Fox	310

Time (in seconds): 0   200   400   600   800   1,000

Test Prep

11 Ahmad left for the fair at 9:30 a.m. He came home at 7:15 p.m. How long was he away?

Ⓐ $9\frac{1}{4}$ hr

Ⓑ $9\frac{3}{4}$ hr

Ⓒ $10\frac{1}{4}$ hr

Ⓓ $10\frac{3}{4}$ hr

12 Complete the table to show equivalent times.

Seconds	Minutes	Hours
	210	
8,400		

13 Select all the times that are equivalent to 450 minutes.

Ⓐ 2,700 seconds

Ⓑ 27,000 seconds

Ⓒ 7 hours 30 minutes

Ⓓ $7\frac{1}{3}$ hours

Ⓔ $7\frac{1}{2}$ hours

Spiral Review

14 Julie decides to use $\frac{1}{3}$ of her gift budget to buy presents for her 4 nieces. She spends the same amount for each niece. How much of her budget does she spend for each niece?

15 A piece of plywood that is 12 inches wide is cut into strips that are $\frac{1}{2}$ inch wide. How many strips of this width can be cut?

Understand Thousandths

1 (MP) **Use Tools** A welder measures the thickness
of a piece of steel. The measuring device shows
the thickness in millimeters.

5.899 mm

- Represent the thickness in the chart.

Ones	•	Tenths	Hundredths	Thousandths
	•			

- How does the value of the 9 in the thousandths place compare
  with the value of the 9 in the hundredths place?

_____

2 During a record-setting rainfall, 0.057 inch of rain fell every
minute for 35 minutes. How much rain fell in 10 minutes?

_____

3 Ten same-sized marbles have a mass of 45.6 grams. What is the
mass of one marble?

_____

Write the number that is 10 times as much as the number.

4 318.625 _____   **5** 28.4 _____

6 Write the number that is $\frac{1}{10}$ of 64.97.

_____

7 **Math on the Spot** An atlas beetle is about
0.15 meter long. How does the length of the atlas
beetle compare to the length of a leafcutting bee?

Bee Lengths (in meters)	
Bumblebee	0.018
Carpenter Bee	0.026
Leafcutting Bee	0.015
Orchid Bee	0.027

_____

_____

Test Prep

8 In which number does the digit 9 have a value that is $\frac{1}{10}$ of the value of the digit 9 in 8.097?

(A) 9.807

(B) 7.908

(C) 7.809

(D) 0.897

9 In which number does the digit 3 have a value that is 10 times as much as the value of the digit 3 in 28.037?

(A) 0.347

(B) 5.693

(C) 28.139

(D) 30.246

10 A Toy Spaniel weighs 10.999 pounds. A Great Dane weighs 10 times as much as the Toy Spaniel weighs. How much does the Great Dane weigh?

_____

11 A sign at the aquarium says an exhibit contains 3,107 gallons of water. How many gallons of water are in an exhibit with $\frac{1}{10}$ of that amount?

_____

12 Select all the numbers that are 10 times as much as 0.14 or $\frac{1}{10}$ of 0.14.

(A) 1.4

(B) 0.014

(C) 14

(D) 0.14

(E) 140

Spiral Review

13 Subtract.

$\frac{2}{3} - \frac{6}{12} =$ _____

14 Find the product.

$\frac{4}{5} \times 3 =$ _____

Name _____

LESSON 13.2
**More Practice/
Homework**

Ed ONLINE
Video Tutorials and
Interactive Examples

Read and Write Decimals to Thousandths

1 An architect's digital tool shows two decimal readings.

- Write the numbers in word form.

   _____

   _____

0.349 m
2.327 m

- Write the numbers in expanded form.

   _____

   _____

2 (MP) **Model with Mathematics** The width of an architect's drawing is 0.985 meter. Write the number in expanded form.

   _____

3 What number is $\frac{1}{100}$ of the value of 2.6? How would you read this number?

   _____

4 Write the number in word form.

351,528.094

   _____

   _____

5 Write the number in expanded form.

4,703.601

   _____

   _____

Test Prep

6 The distance around a human hair is about nine thousandths millimeter. Which number shows the standard form of nine thousandths?

(A) 0.009

(B) 0.09

(C) 9

(D) 9,000

7 Complete the chart for the number 14.097.

Tens	Ones	•	Tenths	Hundredths	Thousandths
1	4	•	0	9	7

1 × 10	4 × 1				
10					

8 Write the number in standard form.

8 × 1 + 5 × 0.1 + 0 × 0.01 + 6 × 0.001

_____

9 Write the number in standard form.

eighty thousand, nine and thirteen thousandths

_____

Spiral Review

10 Write the expression using equivalent fractions with a common denominator.

$2\frac{2}{5} + 3\frac{2}{10}$

11 It took Matt 25 minutes to read a science article. It took him $1\frac{2}{3}$ times as long to read the assigned chapters in a history book. How long did it take Matt to read the history chapters?

Round Decimals

1 (MP) **Attend to Precision** A train travels at the speed shown on the digital readout.

- What is the speed of the train rounded to the nearest tenth?

  _____

- What is the speed of the train rounded to the nearest hundredth?

  _____

123.456
kilometers per hour (kph)

2 A long train carries 74,626,831.08 kilograms of iron ore. What is the mass of this iron ore to the nearest tenth?

_____

Round to the place named.

3 3,854.927 hundredths

_____

4 25.51 ones

_____

5 94.36 tenths

_____

6 683.004 hundredths

_____

7 **Math on the Spot** Mark said that the speed of a housefly rounded to the nearest tenth was 1.9 meters each second. Is he correct? If not, what is his error?

_____

_____

_____

_____

_____

Insect Speeds (meters each second)	
Insect	**Speed**
Dragonfly	6.974
Horsefly	3.934
Bumblebee	2.861
Honeybee	2.548
Housefly	1.967

Test Prep

8 Select all the numbers that round to 6,347.8.

(A) 6,347.751

(B) 6,347.809

(C) 6,347.823

(D) 6,347.852

(E) 6,347.902

9 When diving, a peregrine falcon can reach a speed of 321.869 kilometers each hour. Round this speed to the nearest hundredth and locate it on the number line.

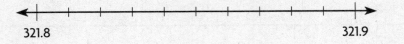

321.8   321.9

10 Numbers are rounded to the nearest tenth and hundredth, as shown in the table. Complete the table to show the numbers that could be rounded.

Number	Rounded to Nearest Tenth	Rounded to Nearest Hundredth
	8.3	8.25
	2.5	2.55
	4.8	4.79

Spiral Review

11 Estimate. Then find the difference.

$5\frac{1}{10} - 1\frac{6}{8}$

Estimate: _____

12 Draw a visual model to find $\frac{1}{4} \times 2$.

Name _____

LESSON 13.4
**More Practice/
Homework**

ONLINE
Ed Video Tutorials and
Interactive Examples

Compare and Order Decimals

1 **STEM** Viscosity is the resistance of a liquid to flow. It describes how quickly a liquid flows. It is measured in units called pascal-seconds (Pa-s). Order the liquids, by name, from greatest to least viscosity.

Viscosities	
Liquid at 25° Celsius	**Viscosity (Pa-s)**
Castor Oil	0.985
Corn Syrup	1.38
Honey	4.5
Olive Oil	0.081

_____

2 Order the numbers from least to greatest.

256.74   256.742   256.472   256.8   256.801

_____

3 Order the numbers from greatest to least.

12.483   12.87   12.9   12.704   12.59

_____

Compare. Write <, >, or =.

4 61.028 ◯ 61.28

5 4,269.381 ◯ 4,269.318

6 932.005 ◯ 932.051

7 21,367.2 ◯ 21,367.02

8 **Math on the Spot** What if the height of Bona Mountain were 0.02 mile greater? Would it then be the mountain with the greatest height? Explain.

Mountains Over Three Miles High	
Mountain and Location	**Height (in miles)**
Blackburn, Alaska	3.104
Bona, Alaska	3.134
Steele, Yukon	3.152

_____

_____

Test Prep

9 The top 4 scores in men's gymnastics for the horizontal bar are shown. The gold medal is given for the highest score. Which score earns the gold medal?

| 15.500 | 15.766 | 15.133 | 15.466 |

(A) 15.500   (C) 15.133

(B) 15.766   (D) 15.466

10 Which are the possible digits that make the statement true? Select all that apply.

$27.864 > 27.8\blacksquare9$

(A) 4

(B) 5

(C) 6

(D) 7

(E) 8

11 Order the numbers from greatest to least.

| 9.754 | 9.75 | 9.574 | 9.7 |

_____

12 Order the numbers from least to greatest.

| 349.5 | 349.27 | 349.216 | 349.02 |

_____

Spiral Review

13 Find the sum.

$\frac{2}{5} + (\frac{2}{3} + \frac{3}{5})$

_____

14 Find the product.

$\frac{4}{5} \times \frac{3}{8}$

_____

LESSON 14.1
**More Practice/
Homework**

ONLINE
Video Tutorials and
Interactive Examples

Represent Decimal Addition

1 (MP) **Critique Reasoning** Eddie uses the quick picture at the right to represent 1.34 + 1.82.

He says the answer is 2.116. Is Eddie correct? Explain your reasoning.

_____

_____

_____

2 (MP) **Use Tools** Joaquin walks 2.54 kilometers to the park and then walks 1.7 kilometers to the store. What is the total distance he walks? Use a quick picture to find your answer.

_____

3 (MP) **Use Tools** Use the decimal model to show the addition of 0.37 and 0.46. Explain how you used the decimal model.

_____

_____

_____

Add. Draw a visual model.

4 0.4 + 0.5 = _____

5 _____ = 0.79 + 0.36

Test Prep

6 Nina buys an apple for $0.58 and an orange for $0.74. How much does she pay for the fruit?

(A) $1.22

(B) $1.32

(C) $1.42

(D) $1.52

7 Ben mixes 0.86 pound of almond flour with 1.39 pounds of coconut flour. What is the total weight?

_____

8 Use the decimal model to show the sum 0.47 + 0.28. What is the sum?

_____

9 Select all the expressions that have a value of 1.64.

(A) 0.86 + 0.88

(B) 0.98 + 0.66

(C) 1.07 + 0.47

(D) 0.29 + 1.35

(E) 0.93 + 0.71

Spiral Review

Convert.

10 72 oz = _____ lb _____ oz

11 134 in. = _____ ft _____ in.

12 Complete the statement. Write *equal to*, *greater than*, or *less than*.

$\frac{3}{2} \times \frac{1}{6}$ is _____ $\frac{1}{6}$.

LESSON 14.2
**More Practice/
Homework**

ONLINE
Video Tutorials and
Interactive Examples

Represent Decimal Subtraction

1 **Math on the Spot** Antonio left his MathBoard on his desk during lunch. The quick picture below shows the problem he was working on when he left.

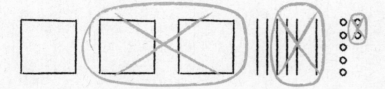

Write a word problem that can be solved using the quick picture, then solve.

_____

_____

2 (MP) **Use Tools** Lin goes on a 4.5-mile hike. After 1 hour, the trail marker shows that she has hiked 3.14 miles. How much farther does she have to hike? Use a quick picture to find your answer.

_____

3 (MP) **Use Tools** A notebook costs $2.35 and a marker costs $1.87. How much more does a notebook cost than a marker? Use a quick picture to find your answer.

_____

4 (MP) **Use Tools** Use the decimal model to show the difference 0.65 − 0.38. What is the difference? Explain how you used the model.

_____

_____

_____

Subtract. Use a visual model.

5 0.8 − 0.3

6 4.5 − 2.3

7 5.3 − 3.86

_____   _____   _____

Test Prep

8 A binder costs $2.68. A book costs $5. How much more does a book cost than a binder?

Ⓐ $2.32

Ⓑ $2.42

Ⓒ $3.32

Ⓓ $3.42

9 Janet has a piece of rope that is 2.33 meters long. She wants to cut the rope so it is 1.5 meters long. How much does she cut off?

_____

10 Use the decimal model to show the difference 0.74 − 0.26. What is the difference?

_____

11 Select all the expressions that have a value of 1.48.

Ⓐ 3.84 − 2.36

Ⓑ 5.74 − 3.26

Ⓒ 4.75 − 3.27

Ⓓ 4.56 − 3.18

Ⓔ 5.27 − 3.79

Spiral Review

Convert.

12 72 in. = _____ yd

13 48 oz = _____ lb

Find the product.

14 $\frac{3}{5} \times \frac{3}{4} =$ _____

15 $\frac{2}{6} \times \frac{4}{8} =$ _____

LESSON 14.3
**More Practice/
Homework**

ONLINE
Video Tutorials and
Interactive Examples

Assess Reasonableness of Sums and Differences

1 **Math on the Spot** Pablo had a cup of shredded wheat cereal, a cup of low-fat milk, and one other item for breakfast. He had about 18 grams of protein. What was the third item Pablo had for breakfast?

Grams of Protein per Serving	
Type of Food	**Protein (in grams)**
1 scrambled egg	6.75
1 cup shredded wheat cereal	5.56
1 oat bran muffin	3.99
1 cup low-fat milk	8.22

_____

2 (MP) **Construct Arguments** The distance from Yolanda's home to Mountaintop School is 8.36 kilometers. Tracy lives 13.85 kilometers farther from the school than Yolanda. Tracy says that she lives about 20 kilometers from school.

- Is Tracy's statement reasonable? Explain.

_____

_____

- How can you find an answer that is closer to the actual distance?

_____

3 (MP) **Model with Mathematics** David buys a sandwich for $5.64 and a carton of milk for $2.19. About how much does David spend? Write an equation to support your answer.

_____

4 (MP) **Use Tools** Nolan says that the difference of 0.81 and 0.23 is 0.58. Is Nolan's statement reasonable? Justify your answer using the number line.

_____

_____

Test Prep

5 A scientist collects two rocks. One rock has a mass of 3.78 kilograms. The other rock has a mass of 8.24 kilograms. Is it reasonable to say that the difference between the masses of the rocks is about 7 kilograms? Explain.

_____

_____

_____

6 Which is a reasonable estimate for the sum 21.34 + 6.45?

Ⓐ 27   Ⓑ 28.5   Ⓒ 29   Ⓓ 32

7 Shakira estimates the sum $14.42 + $9.93. Which could be a reasonable estimate for the sum? Select all that apply.

Ⓐ $20

Ⓑ $22

Ⓒ $24

Ⓓ $24.50

Ⓔ $30

Spiral Review

8 Jenny records the amount of hours she practiced the violin during the week.

$\frac{1}{2}, \frac{1}{2}, \frac{3}{4}, 1, \frac{1}{4}, \frac{1}{4}, \frac{1}{2}$

Show the amounts on the line plot. How much

total time did Jenny practice? _____

9 A rug is $3\frac{1}{4}$ feet long and $1\frac{1}{2}$ feet wide. What is the

area of the rug? _____

Practice Time (hours)

Name _____

LESSON 14.4
**More Practice/
Homework**

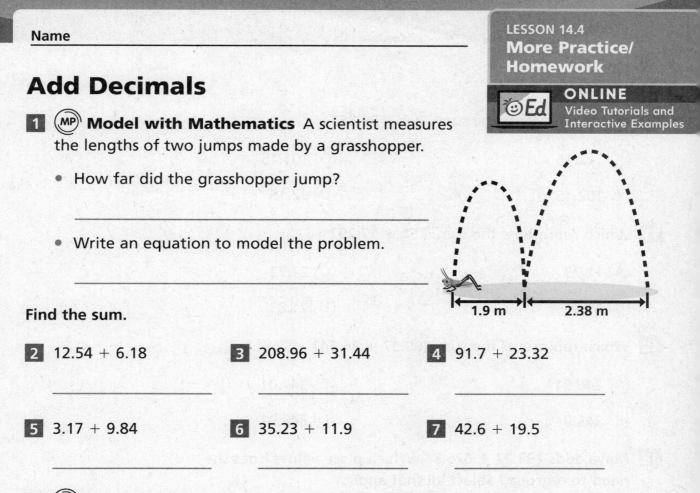

ONLINE
Video Tutorials and
Interactive Examples

Add Decimals

1 (MP) **Model with Mathematics** A scientist measures the lengths of two jumps made by a grasshopper.

- How far did the grasshopper jump?

  _____

- Write an equation to model the problem.

  _____

1.9 m   2.38 m

Find the sum.

2 12.54 + 6.18

_____

3 208.96 + 31.44

_____

4 91.7 + 23.32

_____

5 3.17 + 9.84

_____

6 35.23 + 11.9

_____

7 42.6 + 19.5

_____

8 (MP) **Use Tools** The cost of two magazines is shown in an advertisement. _Horse Health_ costs $4.85, and _World of Ponies_ costs $3.69. What is the cost of both magazines? Use the chart to help you find the cost.

_____

		•	
+		•	

9 **Math on the Spot** Tania measured the growth of her plant each week. The first week, the plant's height measured 2.65 decimeters. During the second week, Tania's plant grew 0.7 decimeter. How tall was Tania's plant at the end of the second week? Describe the steps you took to solve the problem.

_____

_____

_____

_____

_____

Test Prep

10 Which represents the sum 72.3 + 29.85?

Ⓐ 112.15

Ⓒ 101.15

Ⓑ 102.15

Ⓓ 92.15

11 Which represents the sum 4.54 + 17.29?

Ⓐ 11.73

Ⓒ 21.73

Ⓑ 11.83

Ⓓ 21.83

12 Which represents the sum 260.37 + 86.64?

Ⓐ 246.91

Ⓒ 347.01

Ⓑ 346.01

Ⓓ 348.91

13 Maya adds 193.27 + 625.86. Which place values does she need to regroup? Select all that apply.

Ⓐ hundredths

Ⓑ tenths

Ⓒ ones

Ⓓ tens

Ⓔ hundreds

14 An apple costs $1.35 and a carton of juice costs $2.89. What is the cost of an apple and a carton of juice?

_____

Spiral Review

15 Find the end time.

Start time: 6:45 a.m.

Elapsed time: $3\frac{1}{2}$ hr

End time: _____

16 Complete the statement. Write *equal to*, *greater than*, or *less than*.

$\frac{7}{8} \times \frac{5}{8}$ is _____ $\frac{5}{8}$.

LESSON 14.5
**More Practice/
Homework**

 ONLINE
Video Tutorials and
Interactive Examples

Subtract Decimals

1 **Math on the Spot** In peanut butter, how many
more grams of protein are there than grams of
carbohydrates? Use the label at the right.

- Complete each sentence.

  The peanut butter has _____ grams of protein.

  The peanut butter has _____ grams of
  carbohydrates.

- Show how you solved the problem.

  _____

  _____

PEANUT BUTTER	
Nutrition Facts	
Serving Size 2 Tbsp (32.0g)	
Amount Per Serving	
Calories	190
Calories from fat	190
	% Daily Value*
Total Fat 16g	25%
Saturated Fat 3g	18%
Polyunsaturated fat 4.4g	
Monounsaturated fat 7.8g	
Cholesterol 0mg	0%
Sodium 5mg	0%
Total Carbohydrates 6.2g	2%
Dietary Fiber 1.9g	8%
Sugars 2.5g	8%
Protein 8.1g	
*Based on a 2,000 calorie diet	

2 **(MP)** **Attend to Precision** Anna has a sack with 3.55 pounds of
potting soil. She puts 1.8 pounds of the soil in the pot of a rose
plant. How much soil is left in the sack?

_____

Find the difference.

3 $16.41 - 8.72$

4 $5.18 - 2.6$

5 $807.63 - 64.9$

Find the unknown number.

6 $7.8 - \blacksquare = 2.15$

7 $18.69 = \blacksquare - 14.55$

8 $11.26 - 8.4 = \blacksquare$

9 **STEM** The table shows the densities
of the inner planets and the outer
planets. How much more dense is Earth
than Neptune?

Density (g/cm³)	
Inner Planets	**Outer Planets**
Mercury: 5.43	Jupiter: 1.33
Venus: 5.24	Saturn: 0.70
Earth: 5.52	Uranus: 1.30
Mars: 3.94	Neptune: 1.76

© Houghton Mifflin Harcourt Publishing Company

Test Prep

10 Which represents the difference 6.73 − 1.98?

(A) 4.75   (B) 4.85   (C) 5.75   (D) 5.85

11 Which represents the difference 80.05 − 21.4?

(A) 69.65   (B) 68.65   (C) 58.65   (D) 49.65

12 Which represents the difference 132.43 − 88.14?

(A) 54.39   (B) 54.29   (C) 44.39   (D) 44.29

13 William subtracts 381.73 − 163.82. Which place values does he need to regroup? Select all that apply.

(A) hundredths

(B) tenths

(C) ones

(D) tens

(E) hundreds

14 A kite string was 60.3 meters long. After the kite was tangled in a tree, the string was 42.75 meters long. How much string was tangled in the tree?

_____

Spiral Review

15 Jeremy has 21 oranges to divide equally among his friends. If there are 6 people total, how many oranges does each person get?

_____

16 Find the product.

$3\frac{2}{5} \times \frac{3}{4} =$ _____

$2\frac{1}{3} \times 3\frac{4}{6} =$ _____

Name

LESSON 14.6
More Practice/ Homework

 ONLINE
Video Tutorials and
Interactive Examples

Use Strategies and Reasoning to Add and Subtract

1 (MP) **Use Structure** Melissa is solving an addition problem.

$$12.47 + (17.8 + 14.53)$$

- How can Melissa use the Commutative Property of Addition?

  _____

  _____

- How can she use the Associative Property of Addition?

  _____

  _____

- What is the sum?

  _____

2 (MP) **Model with Mathematics** Mr. Smith will buy one of two bookcases. What is the difference in the price of the bookcases? Write an equation using friendly numbers to find the difference.

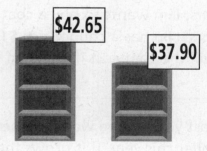

_____

Add or subtract.

3 4.19 + 72.38

4 83.75 − 35.61

_____

5 **Math on the Spot** Lori needs a length of twine 8.5 meters long to mark a row in her garden. Andrew needs a length of twine 7.25 meters long for his row. They have one length of twine that measures 16.27 meters. After they each take the lengths they need, how much twine will be left?

_____

Test Prep

6 What is the value of the expression?

71.34 − 56.25

_____

7 What is the value of the expression?

142.46 + 90.1 + 8.04

_____

8 Which represents the difference 6.79 − 2.43?

Ⓐ 3.36　　　Ⓑ 4.15　　　Ⓒ 4.36　　　Ⓓ 4.46

9 Which represents the sum 4.95 + 13.21?

Ⓐ 17.74　　　Ⓑ 18.16　　　Ⓒ 18.26　　　Ⓓ 18.74

10 Mrs. Lim wants to buy a coat. The coat costs $89.95, but Mrs. Lim has a coupon for $10.50 off the price. How much will the coat cost if Mrs. Lim uses her coupon?

_____

11 Last year, a tree was 12.8 meters tall. It grew 1.35 meters taller this year. If it grows the same amount next year, how tall will the tree be?

_____

Spiral Review

12 Jaime has $\frac{1}{3}$ yard of ribbon to wrap around 2 flowerpots. If he cuts it into equal-sized pieces, how many yards of ribbon does he wrap around each flowerpot?

_____

13 A small dog weighs $6\frac{1}{2}$ pounds. A larger dog weighs $2\frac{2}{3}$ times as much as the small dog. How much does the larger dog weigh?

_____

LESSON 15.1
**More Practice/
Homework**

Ed **ONLINE**
Video Tutorials and
Interactive Examples

Understand Decimal Multiplication Patterns

1 **Financial Literacy** A pence is a unit of currency that is $\frac{1}{100}$ of one British pound. One British pound is worth about $1.30 US. About how much is one pence worth in US currency?

_____

Find the value of the expression.

2 $10^2 \times 827.56$

3 $1,000 \times 62.58$

4 $0.01 \times 47,219$

_____   _____   _____

5 0.01×95.4

6 100×7.39

7 0.1×567.3

_____   _____   _____

Find the value that makes the equation true.

8 $100 \times \blacksquare = 7,285$

9 $685.6 = 0.01 \times \blacksquare$

10 $10 \times \blacksquare = 63.4$

_____   _____   _____

11 Complete the pattern.

$0.01 \times 4,329.8 =$ _____

$0.1 \times 4,329.8 =$ _____

$1 \times 4,329.8 =$ _____

$10 \times 4,329.8 =$ _____

12 Marshal is making punch for a party. He needs to make 100 servings and knows that 1 serving uses 0.75 cup of juice. How much juice will Marshal need?

_____

13 (MP) **Reason** A number is multiplied by 100,000. What happens to the decimal point?

_____

Test Prep

14 Shelby multiplies 7,358.9 by a power of 10 and gets the product 73.589. Select all possible factors.

- (A) $\frac{1}{100}$
- (B) $\frac{1}{10}$
- (C) 1
- (D) 0.1
- (E) 0.01
- (F) 0.001

15 Compare the two expressions. Write <, >, or =.

$10 \times 84.61 \bigcirc \frac{1}{10} \times 8{,}461$

16 Janelle multiplies 728.46 by 10^3. She writes 72,846 as her answer. Is she correct? Explain.

_____

_____

_____

17 Select all the expressions equivalent to 68.4.

- (A) 0.684×100
- (B) 0.684×10^3
- (C) $6.84 \times \frac{1}{10}$
- (D) 6.84×10
- (E) 684×0.01
- (F) $6{,}840 \times \frac{1}{100}$

Spiral Review

18 Compare. Write <, >, or =.

$7.34 \bigcirc 7.034$

19 Add.

$2.475 + 8.2 = $ _____

Represent Multiplication with Decimals and Whole Numbers

1 Baby opossums measure 0.49 inch long at birth. After one month, they triple in length. How long is a one-month-old opossum? _____

Multiply. Use a decimal model.

2 $6 \times 0.15 =$ _____

3 _____ $= 3 \times 0.26$

Multiply. Draw a quick picture.

4 $3 \times 0.58 =$ _____

5 _____ $= 4 \times 0.6$

6 **(MP)** **Model with Mathematics** A toy motorcycle has dimensions scaled from a real motorcycle. The length of the toy is 0.42 foot. To find the length of the real motorcycle, double the length of the toy and then multiply the result by 9. Write equations to model the actual length. What is the length of the real motorcycle?

_____

7 **Math on the Spot** River otters drink about 8 times as much water as a mink drinks in a day. How much water can a river otter drink in 6 days?

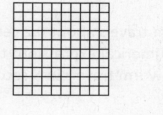

Water Consumption	
Animal	**Average Amount (liters per day)**
Canada Goose	0.24
Cat	0.15
Mink	0.10
Opossum	0.30
Bald Eagle	0.16

© Houghton Mifflin Harcourt Publishing Company

Test Prep

8 A fly measures about 0.25 millimeter in length. A bug is about 3 times as long as the length of the fly. A beetle is about 9 times as long as the length of the bug. Which is closest to the actual length of the beetle?

(A) 0.75 millimeter

(B) 2.25 millimeters

(C) 6.75 millimeters

(D) 12.25 millimeters

9 A small earthworm travels about 0.2 centimeter in 1 second. Select all of the numerical expressions that can be used to find how far the earthworm travels in 5 seconds.

(A) $5 + 0.2$

(B) $0.2 + 0.2 + 0.2 + 0.2 + 0.2$

(C) $5 + 5$

(D) $0.2 + 1 + 5$

(E) 5×0.2

10 Melinda buys 8 party favors. Each favor costs $0.98. How much does Melinda pay?

_____

11 Which is equivalent to the product 5×0.63?

(A) 0.315   (C) 31.5

(B) 3.15   (D) 315

Spiral Review

12 Tamara watched her brother for 4.3 hours today and 3.6 hours yesterday. How many hours did she spend watching her brother?

_____

13 Josh has $4.55 to spend at the store. If he spends $1.25 on a marker, how much does he have left?

_____

Assess Reasonableness of Products

1 During a hurricane, as much as 0.09 inch of rain can fall in 1 minute. Jamal claims that more than 2 inches of rain would fall in 8 minutes. Is Jamal's claim reasonable? Explain.

_____

_____

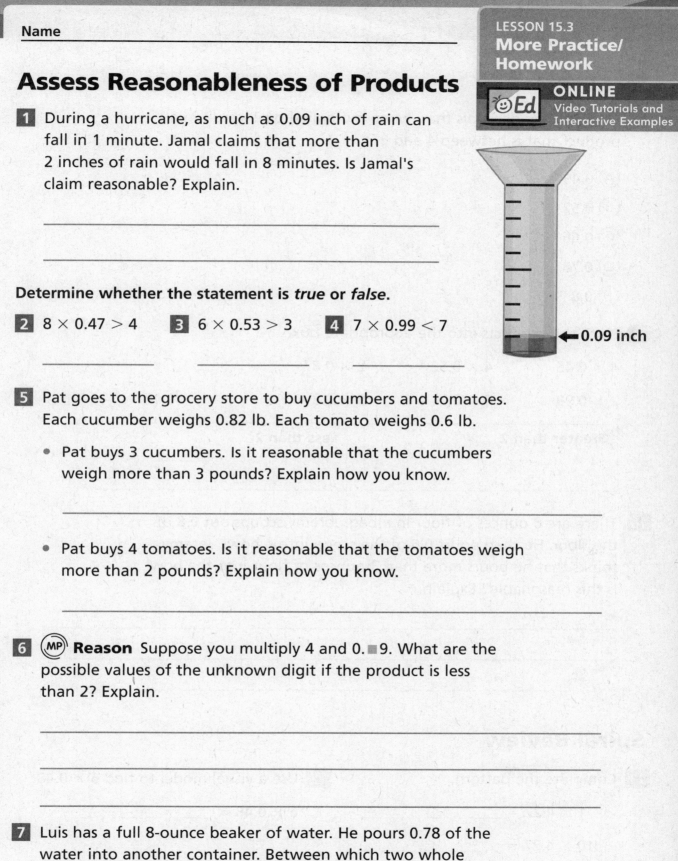

← 0.09 inch

Determine whether the statement is *true* or *false*.

2 $8 \times 0.47 > 4$ **3** $6 \times 0.53 > 3$ **4** $7 \times 0.99 < 7$

_____   _____   _____

5 Pat goes to the grocery store to buy cucumbers and tomatoes. Each cucumber weighs 0.82 lb. Each tomato weighs 0.6 lb.

• Pat buys 3 cucumbers. Is it reasonable that the cucumbers weigh more than 3 pounds? Explain how you know.

_____

• Pat buys 4 tomatoes. Is it reasonable that the tomatoes weigh more than 2 pounds? Explain how you know.

_____

6 (MP) **Reason** Suppose you multiply 4 and 0.■9. What are the possible values of the unknown digit if the product is less than 2? Explain.

_____

_____

_____

7 Luis has a full 8-ounce beaker of water. He pours 0.78 of the water into another container. Between which two whole numbers is the amount of water left in the beaker?

_____

Test Prep

8 Select all the decimals that, when multiplied by 8, result in a product that is between 4 and 6.

Ⓐ 0.49

Ⓑ 0.52

Ⓒ 0.66

Ⓓ 0.78

Ⓔ 0.8

9 Place the products into the appropriate box.

| 4 × 0.48 | 4 × 0.56 | 2 × 0.87 |
| 2 × 0.99 | 4 × 0.7 | 8 × 0.3 |

Greater than 2	Less than 2

10 There are 8 ounces of flour in a bag. Jeremy scoops out 0.8 of the flour. He then pours 0.6 of the scoop into a bowl. Jeremy thinks that he pours more than 3 ounces of flour into the bowl. Is this reasonable? Explain.

_____

_____

_____

Spiral Review

11 Complete the pattern.

1 × 4.27 = _____

10 × 4.27 = _____

100 × 4.27 = _____

1,000 × 4.27 = _____

12 Use a visual model to find 6 × 0.48.

6 × 0.48 = _____

LESSON 15.4
**More Practice/
Homework**

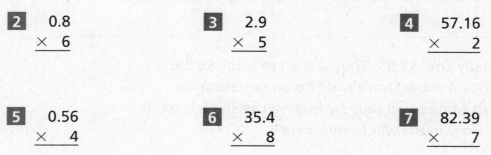

ONLINE
Video Tutorials and
Interactive Examples

Multiply Decimals by 1-Digit Whole Numbers

1 (MP) **Use Tools** Serena can run 6.2 meters in 1 second. How many meters can she run in 7 seconds? Use an area model.

_____

Multiply.

2 0.8
     × 6

3 2.9
     × 5

4 57.16
     ×   2

5 0.56
     ×   4

6 35.4
     ×   8

7 82.39
     ×   7

8 Bob's neighbor pays him $6 each hour to rake leaves. His neighbor says he will pay Bob 1.75 times that amount to mow the lawn. How much will Bob get paid each hour to mow his neighbor's lawn?

_____

9 **Math on the Spot** Chance has $4 in quarters. Blake has $4 in dollar coins. Whose group of coins has the greater mass?

_____

_____

_____

Coin	Mass (in grams)
Nickel	5.00
Dime	2.27
Quarter	5.67
Half-dollar	11.34
Dollar	8.1

Test Prep

10 Dharma multiplies 5.92 and 6. How many digits should be to the right of the decimal point in the product?

- (A) 1
- (B) 2
- (C) 3
- (D) 4

11 Benito claims that the product 9×6.77 is equal to 6.093. Is he correct? Explain.

_____

_____

12 Snow shovels usually cost $9.95. They are on sale for $6.89. Mateo needs to buy 4 snow shovels. Write an equation to model the amount Mateo will save by buying the shovels while they are on sale. How much will Mateo save?

_____

13 Which is the product 9×82.3?

- (A) 73.07
- (B) 74.07
- (C) 730.7
- (D) 740.7

Spiral Review

14 Complete the pattern.

$1 \times 38.72 =$ _____

$10 \times 38.72 =$ _____

$100 \times 38.72 =$ _____

$1,000 \times 38.72 =$ _____

15 Find the unknown number. Use 1 year = 365 days.

7 years = _____ days

Multiply Decimals by 2-Digit Whole Numbers

1 **Math on the Spot** A jacket costs $50 at the store. Evan has a coupon for $15 off. Max pays only 0.6 of the price because his father works at the store. Who will pay the least for the jacket? Explain.

_____

2 A baseball weighs 5.25 ounces. There are 36 baseballs in a bucket. The coach carries the bucket to the field. If the bucket weighs 32 ounces, how many ounces is the coach carrying?

● Draw an area model to find the weight of the baseballs.

● How many ounces is the coach carrying? _____

● Is your answer reasonable? Explain how you know.

_____

_____

_____

Multiply. Show your work.

3   3.1
     × 25

4   0.16
     × 54

5   4.28
     × 92

Test Prep

6 What is the value of 52 × 4.13?

_____

7 Select all the products equal to 20.16.

(A) 48 × 4.2

(B) 48 × 0.42

(C) 14 × 1.44

(D) 14 × 14.4

(E) 21 × 0.96

(F) 16 × 1.26

8 A teacher has a box with 72 pencils. Each pencil weighs
1.6 ounces. What is the total weight of the pencils?

(A) 1,152 ounces

(B) 1,142 ounces

(C) 115.2 ounces

(D) 114.2 ounces

9 Each brick weighs 1.34 pounds. Ann carries 4 bricks. Ben
carries 6 bricks. Calvin carries 7 bricks. What is the total weight
of the bricks?

_____

Spiral Review

10 Convert.

24 qt = _____ gal

75 in. = _____ ft

56 oz = _____ lb

11 Multiply.

4.76 × 9 = _____

4.75 × 6 = _____

5.13 × 8 = _____

Solve Problems Using Bar Models

Use the prices of the items shown for 1 and 2. Draw a bar
model to solve.

$2.79 $16.99

1 How much would it cost to buy 1 soccer ball and
3 cans of tennis balls?

_____

2 How much more does 1 soccer ball cost than
3 cans of tennis balls?

_____

3 **Math on the Spot** It costs $5.25 to rent a kayak for 1 hour
at a local state park. The price per hour stays the same for
up to 6 hours of rental. After 6 hours, the cost decreases to
$4.50 per hour. How much would it cost to rent a kayak
for 8 hours?

_____

Test Prep

4 Mr. Green is 6 feet tall. He planted a tree that was 1.45 feet tall. After a year, its height tripled. How much taller is Mr. Green than the tree?

_____

5 Mrs. Green's vegetable garden was 2.25 meters long. After a year, she doubled its length. After another year, she made it 1.75 meters longer. How long is Mrs. Green's vegetable garden?

_____

6 Aaron buys 5 notebooks that cost $1.49 each. If Aaron pays with a $10 bill, how much change should he receive?

Ⓐ $2.55

Ⓑ $2.65

Ⓒ $3.45

Ⓓ $4.55

Spiral Review

7 Multiply.

$5 \times 56.3 =$ _____

$9 \times 7.33 =$ _____

$7 \times 42.68 =$ _____

$4 \times 193.46 =$ _____

8 Convert.

9 lb = _____ oz

$4\frac{1}{2}$ yd = _____ in.

28 in. = _____ ft

42 c = _____ qt

LESSON 16.1
**More Practice/
Homework**

 ONLINE
Video Tutorials and
Interactive Examples

Represent Decimal Multiplication

1 (MP) **Use Tools** Edgar has a collection of stickers. Of his stickers, 0.2 are circle shaped. Of those circle-shaped stickers, 0.6 have words on them. What part of his collection, expressed as a decimal, is circle shaped with words on them?

- Write a multiplication expression that models the situation.

  _____

- Use the decimal model to find this part of his collection. Explain how you used the model.

  _____

  _____

Find the area of the rectangle for the given dimensions. Use the decimal model.

2 length = 0.7 mm
width = 0.6 mm

area = _____

3 length = 0.7 cm
width = 1.5 cm

area = _____

4 **Math on the Spot** Randy and Stacy used models to find 0.4 of 0.6. Both Randy's and Stacy's models are shown. Whose model makes sense? Whose model is nonsense? Explain.

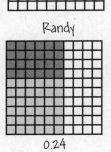

Randy

Stacy

0.24   1.0

_____

_____

_____

_____

Test Prep

5 What is the value of 0.5 × 0.9? Use the decimal model.

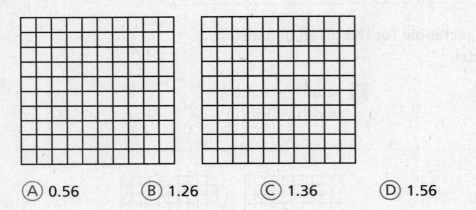

---

6 Which is the value of 0.8 × 1.7? Use the decimal model.

(A) 0.56   (B) 1.26   (C) 1.36   (D) 1.56

7 Select all the expressions that have a value of 0.48.

(A) 0.4 × 1.2

(B) 4 × 1.2

(C) 0.6 × 0.8

(D) 6 × 0.8

(E) 0.6 × 8

Spiral Review

8 Convert.

130 in. = _____ ft _____ in.

80 oz = _____ lb _____ oz

9 Multiply.

9.286 × 10 = _____

293.23 × $\frac{1}{10}$ = _____

LESSON 16.2
**More Practice/
Homework**

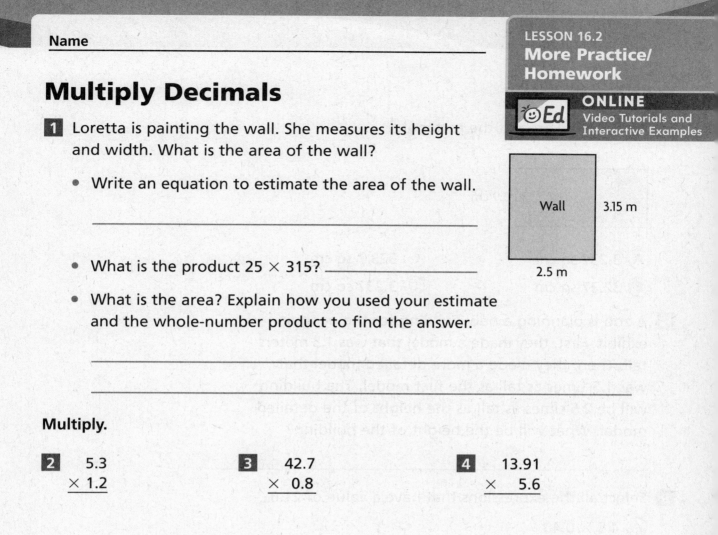

ONLINE
Video Tutorials and
Interactive Examples

Multiply Decimals

1 Loretta is painting the wall. She measures its height and width. What is the area of the wall?

- Write an equation to estimate the area of the wall.

_____

- What is the product 25 × 315? _____

- What is the area? Explain how you used your estimate and the whole-number product to find the answer.

_____

_____

Wall   3.15 m

2.5 m

Multiply.

2   5.3
   × 1.2

3   42.7
   × 0.8

4   13.91
   × 5.6

5 **STEM** The moon has less mass than Earth. So the effect of the moon's gravity on the weight of an object is less than the Earth's. An object that weighs 1 pound on Earth weighs only 0.17 pound on the moon. Suppose a rock brought back from the moon weighs 2.5 pounds on Earth. What would the rock weigh

on the moon? _____

6 (MP) **Critique Reasoning** Arthur claims 0.4 × 2.35 = 9.4. He reasons that 4 × 235 = 940, and since 4 differs from 0.4 by 1 decimal place value and 235 differs from 2.35 by 2 decimal place values, the product differs from the whole-number product by 2 decimal place values since it is the greater number. Is Arthur correct? Explain.

_____

_____

Test Prep

7 Which is the area of the rectangle?

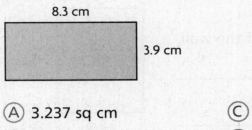

8.3 cm

3.9 cm

(A) 3.237 sq cm

(C) 323.7 sq cm

(B) 32.37 sq cm

(D) 3,237 sq cm

8 A zoo is planning a new building for the penguin exhibit. First, they made a model that was 1.3 meters tall. Then, they made a more detailed model that was 1.5 times as tall as the first model. The building will be 2.5 times as tall as the height of the detailed model. What will be the height of the building?

_____

9 Select all the expressions that have a value of 21.6.

(A) 4.5 × 0.48

(B) 4.5 × 4.8

(C) 1.8 × 12

(D) 1.6 × 1.35

(E) 1.6 × 13.5

(F) 0.3 × 6.48

Spiral Review

10 Fred jumped 2 yards 1 foot. Greg jumped 5 feet 30 inches. Who jumped farther? How much farther?

11 Write the decimal in word form.

246.829

_____

_____

Name _____

LESSON 16.3
**More Practice/
Homework**

Ed **ONLINE**
Video Tutorials and
Interactive Examples

Multiply Decimals with Zeros in the Product

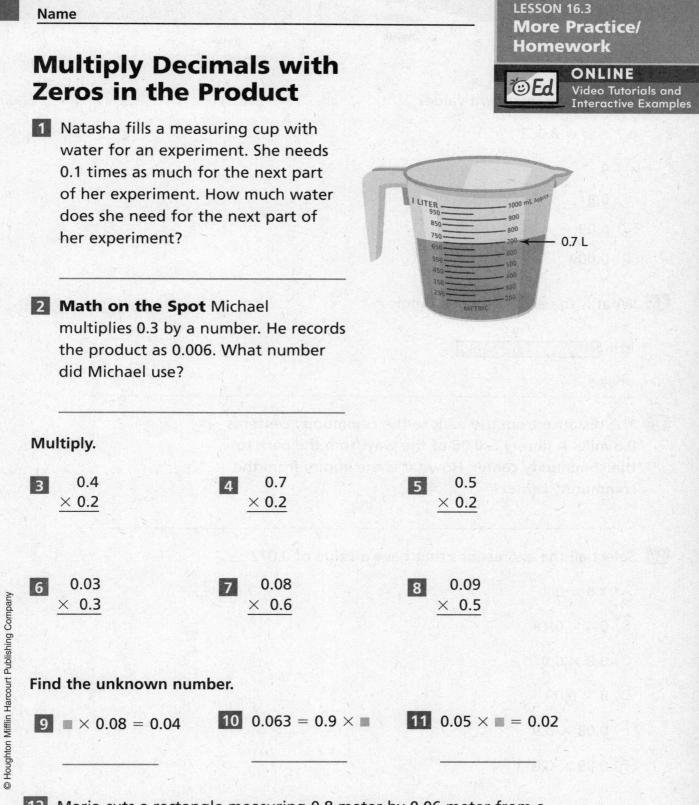

1 Natasha fills a measuring cup with water for an experiment. She needs 0.1 times as much for the next part of her experiment. How much water does she need for the next part of her experiment?

0.7 L

_____

2 **Math on the Spot** Michael multiplies 0.3 by a number. He records the product as 0.006. What number did Michael use?

_____

Multiply.

3 $\begin{array}{r} 0.4 \\ \times\ 0.2 \\ \hline \end{array}$

4 $\begin{array}{r} 0.7 \\ \times\ 0.2 \\ \hline \end{array}$

5 $\begin{array}{r} 0.5 \\ \times\ 0.2 \\ \hline \end{array}$

6 $\begin{array}{r} 0.03 \\ \times\ 0.3 \\ \hline \end{array}$

7 $\begin{array}{r} 0.08 \\ \times\ 0.6 \\ \hline \end{array}$

8 $\begin{array}{r} 0.09 \\ \times\ 0.5 \\ \hline \end{array}$

Find the unknown number.

9 ■ × 0.08 = 0.04

10 0.063 = 0.9 × ■

11 0.05 × ■ = 0.02

_____   _____   _____

12 Maria cuts a rectangle measuring 0.8 meter by 0.06 meter from a sheet of paper. What is the area of the rectangle?

_____

Test Prep

13 Which is the unknown value?

$0.7 \times \blacksquare = 0.063$

(A) 9

(B) 0.9

(C) 0.09

(D) 0.009

14 What is the area of the rectangle?

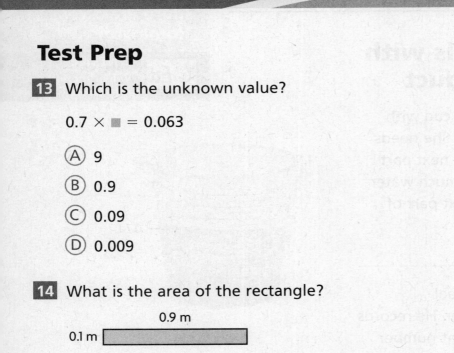

0.9 m

0.1 m

_____

15 The distance from the park to the community center is 0.8 mile. A library is 0.06 of the way from the park to the community center. How far is the library from the community center?

_____

16 Select all the expressions that have a value of 0.072.

(A) 1.8×0.4

(B) 0.4×0.18

(C) 0.8×0.9

(D) 8×0.09

(E) 0.08×0.9

(F) 0.09×0.8

Spiral Review

17 Convert.

650 sec = _____ min _____ sec

18 Round 289.353 to the nearest tenth.

_____

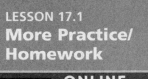
Understand Decimal Division Patterns

1 The shipment holds 100 bottles of glue.

- Use a pattern to find the weight of one bottle of glue.

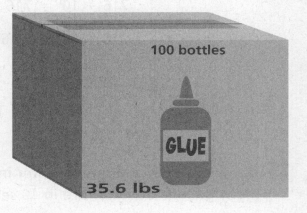

100 bottles

GLUE

35.6 lbs

- What is the weight of one bottle of glue?

_____

2 (MP) **Attend to Precision** If each muffin contains the same amount of sugar, how many kilograms of sugar are in each corn muffin?

Dry Ingredients for 1,000 Corn Muffins	
Ingredient	Number of Kilograms
Cornmeal	150
Flour	110
Sugar	66
Baking powder	10
Salt	4

_____

Complete the pattern.

3 $45 \div 1 =$ _____

$45 \div 10 =$ _____

$45 \div 100 =$ _____

4 $38 \div 10^0 =$ _____

$38 \div 10^1 =$ _____

$38 \div 10^2 =$ _____

$38 \div 10^3 =$ _____

5 $110 \div 10^0 =$ _____

$110 \div 10^1 =$ _____

$110 \div 10^2 =$ _____

$110 \div 10^3 =$ _____

6 $693 \div 1 =$ _____

$693 \div 10 =$ _____

$693 \div 100 =$ _____

$693 \div 1,000 =$ _____

Test Prep

7 Compete the pattern. What is the next number?

$$716 \div 10^0 = 716$$
$$716 \div 10^1 = 71.6$$
$$716 \div 10^2 = \blacksquare$$

(A) 0.0716
(B) 0.716
(C) 7.16
(D) 71.6

8 If there are 826 gallons of water in 1,000 servings, how many gallons of water are in 10 servings?

(A) 8,260 gallons
(B) 82.6 gallons
(C) 8.26 gallons
(D) 0.826 gallon

9 Select all of the numbers that make the equation true.

$$827 \div \blacksquare = 0.827$$

(A) 1,000
(B) 100
(C) 10
(D) 10^3
(E) 10^2

10 Tell how many places and in what direction you should shift the decimal point to find the quotient $79 \div 100$.

_____

Spiral Review

11 Add. Draw a quick picture.

$2.26 + 1.05 = $ _____

12 Multiply. Draw a quick picture.

$3 \times 0.46 = $ _____

© Houghton Mifflin Harcourt Publishing Company

Represent Division of Decimals by Whole Numbers

1 A box contains 5 toy cars. If the weight of each car is the same, how much does one toy car weigh?

- Use quick pictures to represent the problem.

TOY CARS

7.15 lbs

- How much does each toy car weigh? _____

2 Seana has a rope that is 42.5 yards long. She cuts it into 5 equal pieces for games of tug-of-war. How long is each piece of rope?

_____

3 **Math on the Spot** Aida is making banners from a roll of paper that is 5.04 meters long. She will cut the paper into 4 equal lengths. She uses base-ten blocks to model how long each piece will be. Describe Aida's error.

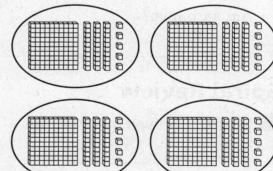

_____

_____

_____

_____

Divide.

4 $5.2 \div 4 =$ _____   **5** _____ $= 8.6 \div 2$ **6** $9.5 \div 5 =$ _____

Test Prep

7 Divide.

$7.6 \div 4 = \blacksquare$

_____

8 Gina buys 7 tacos for $4.20. How much does each taco cost?

(A) $0.51

(B) $0.60

(C) $0.61

(D) $0.70

9 There are 29.6 feet of carpet in a roll at the store. If it were cut into 8 equal pieces, what would be the length of each piece?

_____

10 Fletcher runs 4 miles in 37.60 minutes. He runs each mile in the same amount of time. How long does it take him to run each mile?

_____

Spiral Review

11 Subtract. Draw a quick picture.

$3.14 - 1.7 = $ _____

12 Determine whether the statement is _true_ or _false_.

$6 \times 0.32 > 3$ _____

$9 \times 0.72 < 6$ _____

Assess Reasonableness of Quotients

1 (MP) **Reason** A geologist collects a soil sample that weighs 43.5 ounces. The geologist wants to place an equal amount of soil into each jar for separate testing. About how much soil does the geologist place in each jar?

- Write a division expression for the problem.

  _____

- Rename the dividend as a number of tenths, and adjust it to be a compatible number with 6.

  _____

- Estimate the quotient. About how much soil is placed in each jar?

  _____

2 **Math on the Spot** The greatest monthly snowfall total in Alaska is 297.9 inches. This happened in February, 1953. Compare the daily average snowfall for February, 1953, with the average daily snowfall for Alaska's greatest 7-day snowfall. Use estimation.

Greatest 7-Day Snowfall	
State	**Amount of Snow (in inches)**
Alaska	186.9
Wyoming	84.5
South Dakota	112.7

_____

_____

_____

Estimate the quotient by using compatible numbers.

3 237.6 ÷ 8

Dividend: _____

Divisor: _____

Quotient: _____

4 358.9 ÷ 7

Dividend: _____

Divisor: _____

Quotient: _____

Test Prep

5 Which number is closest to the actual quotient?

$4.82 \div 7 = \blacksquare$

(A) 7

(B) 6

(C) 0.7

(D) 0.6

6 Mandie has 3.8 liters of lemonade. She pours the same amount of lemonade into 8 pitchers. Which is closest to the actual number of liters of lemonade that she pours into each pitcher?

(A) 2 liters

(B) 1 liter

(C) 0.5 liter

(D) 0.25 liter

7 A park district buys some sporting equipment for $1,084.56. They agree to make 12 equal payments over one year. Is it reasonable that they expect to pay about $100 each month? Explain.

_____

_____

_____

Spiral Review

8 Jon earns $3 for every package he wraps. To take a package to the post office, Jon earns 1.65 times as much as he earns for wrapping a package. How much will Jon earn for wrapping a package and taking it to the post office?

_____

9 Jordana buys a salad at the store for $4.35. How much change does she receive if she pays with a $10 bill?

Divide Decimals by Whole Numbers

1 (MP) **Use Tools** Some campers go out to collect water from a stream. They share the water equally among 8 campsites. How much water does each campsite get?

- Estimate the quotient.

_____

_____

- Make a quick picture to show 8 equal groups.

Water
62.4 liters

- How much water does each campsite get?

_____

- Is your answer reasonable? Explain.

_____

_____

2 Mei runs the same distance 6 days each week. In 4 weeks, she runs 151.68 miles. How many miles does Mei run each day?

_____

Divide.

3 5)46.5

4 8)32.8

5 4)63.6

6 13)92.3

7 24)415.2

8 45)552.15

Test Prep

9 Mia rides her bike 18.5 miles in 5 days. If she rides her bike the same number of miles each day, how many miles does she ride in one day? Describe how you can use a quick picture to find your answer.

_____

_____

_____

_____

10 Dolly buys 12 identical pens for $9.48. How much does each pen cost?

_____

11 A group of 23 friends pays $293.25 for tickets to a show. If each ticket is the same price, what is the price of each ticket?

_____

12 Tommy goes to lunch with his coworkers and the bill is $58.92. If they divide the bill equally 3 ways, how much will each person pay?

Ⓐ $14.73
Ⓑ $18.64
Ⓒ $19.54
Ⓓ $19.64

Spiral Review

13 Add.

$35.6 + 2.63 =$ _____

$5.87 + 0.9 =$ _____

14 Multiply.

$35 \times 2.6 =$ _____

$28 \times 0.68 =$ _____

LESSON 17.5
**More Practice/
Homework**

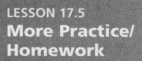

 ONLINE
Video Tutorials and
Interactive Examples

Represent Decimal Division

1 (MP) **Use Tools** Georgie has $2.45 to spend on hot chocolate packets. Each packet costs $0.35. How many packets can Georgie buy?

• Use decimal models to show the dividend.

• Use your decimal model to find the quotient.

_____

Identify the dividend and divisor in each problem. Then solve.

2 A small art paintbrush costs $0.95. If Jaime has $4.75, how many brushes can she buy?

Dividend: _____

Divisor: _____

_____

3 Rick is making new shelves for his room. He has 20.4 feet of wood. If he needs 3.4 feet of wood for each shelf, how many shelves can he make?

Dividend: _____

Divisor: _____

_____

Use decimal models to find each quotient.

4 $1.6 \div 0.8 =$ _____

5 $0.9 \div 0.3 =$ _____

Test Prep

6 Samara pays $1.12 for some beads. Each bead costs $0.16. Which expression models the number of beads Samara buys?

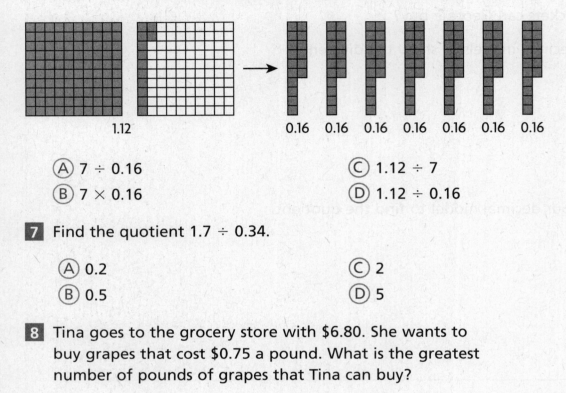

1.12   0.16 0.16 0.16 0.16 0.16 0.16 0.16

Ⓐ 7 ÷ 0.16

Ⓑ 7 × 0.16

Ⓒ 1.12 ÷ 7

Ⓓ 1.12 ÷ 0.16

7 Find the quotient 1.7 ÷ 0.34.

Ⓐ 0.2

Ⓑ 0.5

Ⓒ 2

Ⓓ 5

8 Tina goes to the grocery store with $6.80. She wants to buy grapes that cost $0.75 a pound. What is the greatest number of pounds of grapes that Tina can buy?

Ⓐ 8 pounds

Ⓑ 8.5 pounds

Ⓒ 9 pounds

Ⓓ 9.5 pounds

9 Use a decimal model to find the quotient 2.7 ÷ 0.9.

_____

Spiral Review

10 Three hours ago, Otto's digital thermometer showed that the temperature outside was 74.8 degrees. Now, the thermometer shows that the temperature is 54.9 degrees. By how much did the temperature drop?

_____

11 Multiply. Use the decimal model.

0.4 × 0.6 = _____

LESSON 17.6
**More Practice/
Homework**

ONLINE
Video Tutorials and
Interactive Examples

Divide Decimals

1 Marcus wants to go hiking while he is on vacation.
The trail is 2.76 miles long, and Marcus hikes
0.46 mile each hour. How long will it take him to
hike the entire trail?

_____

2 Sami is making necklaces for a craft show. Each
necklace is 33.4 centimeters long. If she has
233.8 centimeters of cord, how many necklaces
can Sami make?

_____

3 **Math on the Spot** Ramon paid $3.25 for notepads
and $1.44 for markers. What is the total number of
items he bought?

Prices at School Store	
Item	**Price**
Eraser	$0.05
Marker	$0.36
Notepad	$0.65
Pencil	$0.12

_____

4 (MP) **Model with Mathematics** A box of pasta weighs
13.6 ounces. A recipe calls for 95.2 ounces of pasta.
Write and solve an equation to find the number of
boxes of pasta needed to make the recipe.

_____

Divide.

5 17.36 ÷ 2.8

6 135.7 ÷ 5.9

7 206.64 ÷ 24.6

_____

8 320.4 ÷ 8.9

9 221.52 ÷ 7.8

10 502.55 ÷ 11.5

_____

Test Prep

11 Mia pays $3.15 for new red pencils. If they cost $0.45 each, how many red pencils does Mia buy?

_____

12 Jesse calculates 89.24 ÷ 2.3 and gets an answer of 388. What error might Jesse have made?

(A) He forgot to regroup when he was dividing.

(B) He forgot to place the decimal point: 38.8.

(C) He should have rounded his answer.

(D) He should have written a decimal point: 3.88.

13 Which is the quotient 874.92 ÷ 13.8?

(A) 63.9

(B) 63.4

(C) 6.39

(D) 6.34

14 Divide.

19.6 ÷ 1.4

_____

Spiral Review

15 Find the sum or difference.

13.4 + 3.2 + 1.1

_____

9.88 − 2.4

_____

16 Find the product.

6.4 × 3.5

_____

8.72 × 5.6

_____

LESSON 17.7
**More Practice/
Homework**

ONLINE
⊙Ed Video Tutorials and
Interactive Examples

Write Zeros in the Dividend

1 Maple has 4 identical loaves of bread that weigh
a total of 6.6 pounds. How much does 1 loaf of
bread weigh?

_____

2 **(MP)** **Model with Mathematics** Murph has a box where he
keeps shells that he collects from the beach. When the box
was empty, it weighed 43 ounces. Now that it is full of shells,
it weighs 668.3 ounces. If Murph has 74 shells that are similar in
weight, about how many ounces does each shell weigh? Write
and solve an equation to model this situation.

_____

_____

3 **Math on the Spot** Amy has 3 pounds of raisins. She divides the
raisins equally into 12 bags. How many pounds of raisins are in
each bag? Tell how many zeros you had to write at the end of
the dividend to solve.

_____

4 Hal was buying crafts for a school project. He
bought a few fabric squares and spent $22.05.
Write an equation to model the situation.
How many fabric squares did Hal buy?

Craft Supply Price List	
Item	**Price**
Ribbon	$1.43
Glitter tubes	$0.95
Glue sticks	$0.65
Fabric squares	$2.45

_____

Divide.

5 $0.84 \div 2.4$ **6** $2.32 \div 0.16$ **7** $20.7 \div 3.6$

Test Prep

8 Sherman has a rope that is 14.2 feet long. He cuts it into 4 equal pieces. How long is each piece of rope?

   Ⓐ 3.46 feet

   Ⓑ 3.52 feet

   Ⓒ 3.55 feet

   Ⓓ 4.52 feet

9 The area of a rectangular tabletop is 23.8 square feet. The tabletop is 4.25 feet wide. How long is the tabletop?

_____

10 Divide.

97.3 ÷ 35

_____

11 Misty divides 38.88 ounces of popcorn kernels equally into 6 bags. How many ounces of kernels does she put in each bag?

   Ⓐ 6.82 ounces

   Ⓑ 6.48 ounces

   Ⓒ 6.32 ounces

   Ⓓ 5.148 ounces

Spiral Review

12 What is the product of 0.6 and 0.03?

_____

13 Shen's maple tree was 2.48 meters high when she planted it. After one year, the tree doubled in height. After another year, the tree tripled its height from the previous year. How tall is Shen's tree? Use a bar model to solve.

_____

LESSON 18.1
**More Practice/
Homework**

ONLINE
Video Tutorials and
Interactive Examples

Understand Metric Conversions

1 (MP) **Model with Mathematics** An ice cream cone with a height of about 16 centimeters has a liquid volume of about 0.268 liter. Write the cone's height in meters and its liquid volume in milliliters in the table. Insert a decimal point in both answers.

height							
liquid volume							
	kilo-	hecto-	deka-	meter liter gram	deci-	centi-	milli-

2 A chihuahua that has a mass of about 1,107 grams at 8 weeks of age will have a mass of about 3.715 kilograms when fully grown.

- About how many kilograms is the mass of the chihuahua at 8 weeks of age? _____

- About how many grams is the mass of the chihuahua when fully grown? _____

3 Write each of the dimensions of the flag in meters.

_____

_____

_____

_____

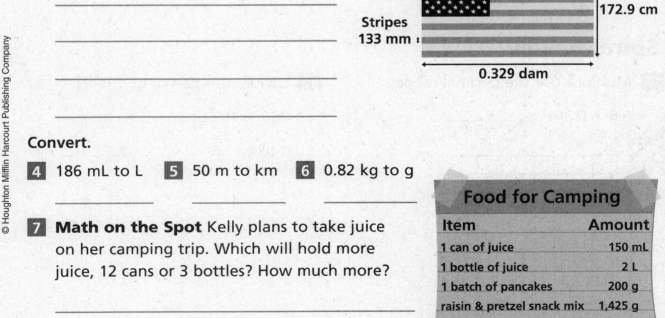

13.18 dm

172.9 cm

Stripes
133 mm

0.329 dam

Convert.

4 186 mL to L   **5** 50 m to km   **6** 0.82 kg to g

_____   _____   _____

7 **Math on the Spot** Kelly plans to take juice on her camping trip. Which will hold more juice, 12 cans or 3 bottles? How much more?

_____

_____

Food for Camping	
Item	**Amount**
1 can of juice	150 mL
1 bottle of juice	2 L
1 batch of pancakes	200 g
raisin & pretzel snack mix	1,425 g

Test Prep

8 Each day, a Florida resident uses about 515,000 milliliters of water. About how many liters of water is this?

- (A) 0.515 liter
- (B) 5.15 liters
- (C) 515 liters
- (D) 515,000 liters

9 The smallest bone in the human body is the stapes bone in the middle ear. It measures 2.8 millimeters long. What is the length of the stapes bone in centimeters?

_____

10 Select all of the measurement conversions in which the decimal point is shifted to the left.

- (A) decimeters to dekameters
- (B) dekaliters to deciliters
- (C) hectograms to centigrams
- (D) centiliters to hectoliters
- (E) decigrams to milligrams

Spiral Review

11 Multiply. Use the decimal model.

$0.8 \times 0.3 =$ _____

12 Divide. Use partial quotients.

$236 \div 16$ _____

$1,924 \div 38$ _____

LESSON 18.2
**More Practice/
Homework**

 ONLINE
Video Tutorials and
Interactive Examples

Solve Customary and Metric Conversion Problems

1 (MP) **Attend to Precision** The recently discovered fossil of an ancient bird revealed that it had a giant wingspan. What was the approximate wingspan of the bird in centimeters and in millimeters?

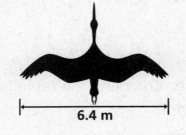

6.4 m

_____

2 A bird's egg weighs 4 ounces. What is the weight of the egg in pounds?

_____

3 The elevation of the highest natural point in Florida is 345 feet.

- What is this height in inches?

  _____

- What is this height in yards?

  _____

Convert.

4 52 mL to L   **5** 5 qt to gal   **6** 750 g to kg

_____   _____   _____

7 A water bottle holds 375 milliliters of water. How many liters does the bottle hold?

_____

Test Prep

8 Scientists have found a species of fish that swims at a depth of about 4.96 miles in the Pacific Ocean's Mariana Trench. About how many feet is the swimming depth of these fish?

- (A) 178.56 ft
- (B) 2,142.72 ft
- (C) 8,729.6 ft
- (D) 26,188.8 ft

9 A container can hold 13 quarts. Complete the table for the liquid volume of the container.

gal	qt	pt	c

10 A frog hops 45 centimeters 6 times in a row. How many meters does the frog jump?

- (A) 270 meters
- (B) 27 meters
- (C) 2.7 meters
- (D) 0.27 meter

11 Kendra uses a 1-pint measuring cup to fill a container. After the 36th time, the container is full with no liquid spilled. How many gallons of liquid are in the container?

- (A) 18 gallons
- (B) 9 gallons
- (C) 4.5 gallons
- (D) 2.25 gallons

Spiral Review

12 Multiply.

8.4
$\times$ 2.3

13 Divide.

$452 \div 31$

Name _____

LESSON 18.3
**More Practice/
Homework**

ⓔEd **ONLINE**
Video Tutorials and
Interactive Examples

Solve Multistep Measurement Problems

1 Jen mixes $1\frac{1}{2}$ cups of mango juice, $1\frac{1}{2}$ pints of pineapple juice, and $1\frac{1}{8}$ quarts of orange juice to make a fruit punch. How many quarts of fruit punch does Jen make?

_____

2 (MP) **Use Tools** Josiah ties together two strings. One string is $3\frac{3}{4}$ feet long. The other string is $1\frac{1}{2}$ yards long. The knot he makes to tie the strings subtracts $2\frac{1}{2}$ inches from the total length. Mark the length, in inches, of the two tied strings on the number line.

76 77 78 79 80 81 82 83 84 85 86 87 88 89 90 91 92 93 94 95 96 97 98 99 100

3 One batch of a recipe calls for 185 grams of whole-wheat flour, 0.115 kilogram of pastry flour, and 100 grams of bread flour. How many kilograms of flour are needed for 3 batches?

- How do you convert a number of grams to a number of kilograms?

_____

- How many kilograms of flour are needed for 3 batches?

_____

4 **Math on the Spot** Maria puts trim around a mirror that is in the shape of a square. Each side is 24 inches long. Maria has 1 foot of trim left. What was the length of the trim when she started? Write your answer in yards.

_____

Test Prep

5 Half-dollar coins weigh 4 ounces and quarters weigh
0.2 pound. Laurel has 9 half-dollar coins and 25 quarters in
her coin bank. Her coin bank weighs 2 pounds. Laurel lifts the
coin bank. How much does the bank and the coins weigh?

   (A) 43 ounces   (C) 118 ounces

   (B) 88 ounces   (D) 148 ounces

6 The base of one of the monuments in Gettysburg, Pennsylvania,
measures about 3,500 millimeters by 140 centimeters.
What is the area of the monument's base in square meters?

_____

7 To make punch for a party, Jamir mixes three 375-milliliter
bottles of apple juice, two 750-milliliter bottles of grape
juice, and one 1.375-liter bottle of seltzer water. How many
liters of punch does he have?

_____

8 Haley is returning from a business trip. Her empty suitcase
has a mass of 5.1 kg. Her clothes have a combined mass of
14.8 kg. Haley also wants to pack 4 gifts, each with a mass
of 870 g. The airline restriction for a suitcase is a limit of
22.7 kg. Can Haley bring everything home in her suitcase?
If not, how many gifts can she pack? Explain.

_____

_____

_____

Spiral Review

9 Multiply.

    0.06
  × 0.4
  _____

10 Evaluate the numerical expression.

$$(12 - 4) \times (2 + 4)$$

_____

LESSON 19.1
**More Practice/
Homework**

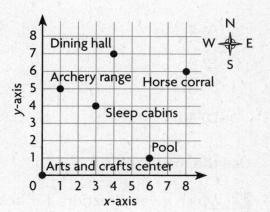
ONLINE
Video Tutorials and
Interactive Examples

Describe a Coordinate System

1 The map shows the locations of the different
activities at a camp.

- What are two ways to name the location of
  the arts and crafts center

  _____

  _____

- Using the map, describe how a camper
  would go from the arts and crafts center to
  the dining hall.

  _____

- What ordered pair represents the location
  of the horse corral?

  _____

**Describe how to move from the origin of a coordinate grid to locate
the point.**

2 $A(2, 8)$

_____

_____

3 $B(4, 0)$

_____

_____

4 $C(9, 5)$

_____

_____

5 (MP) **Use Structure** Nathan says that Madison
Square Garden is located at (0, 3) on the map.
Is his ordered pair correct? Explain.

_____

_____

_____

_____

_____

Map of New York City

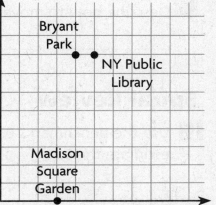

Test Prep

6 A point is located 6 units right and 4 units up from the origin. What is the x-coordinate of the point?

(A) 2

(B) 4

(C) 6

(D) 10

Use the map for 7–10.

7 Which gives directions for how to move from the origin to the cafe?

(A) right 3 units, up 5 units

(B) right 5 units, up 3 units

(C) right 4 units, up 2 units

(D) right 1 unit, up 3 units

8 What are the coordinates of the bank?

_____

9 What is located at (7, 2) on the map?

_____

10 Describe how to move from the origin to the store.

_____

Spiral Review

11 Use the benchmarks 0, $\frac{1}{2}$, and 1 to estimate the sum.

$\frac{1}{5} + \frac{3}{8}$

_____

12 A machine in a candy factory can make 62 candies in one hour. About how long would it take to make 2,480 candies?

_____

LESSON 19.2
**More Practice/
Homework**

ONLINE
Video Tutorials and
Interactive Examples

Understand Ordered Pairs

**Each unit on the coordinate grid represents
1 mile. Use the coordinate grid for 1 and 2.**

1 The parking lot is located at (4, 6). Plot the
parking lot on the coordinate grid. Explain
how you plotted the point.

_____

_____

2 **Reason** Is the parking lot closer to the cabin or
the lake? Explain.

_____

_____

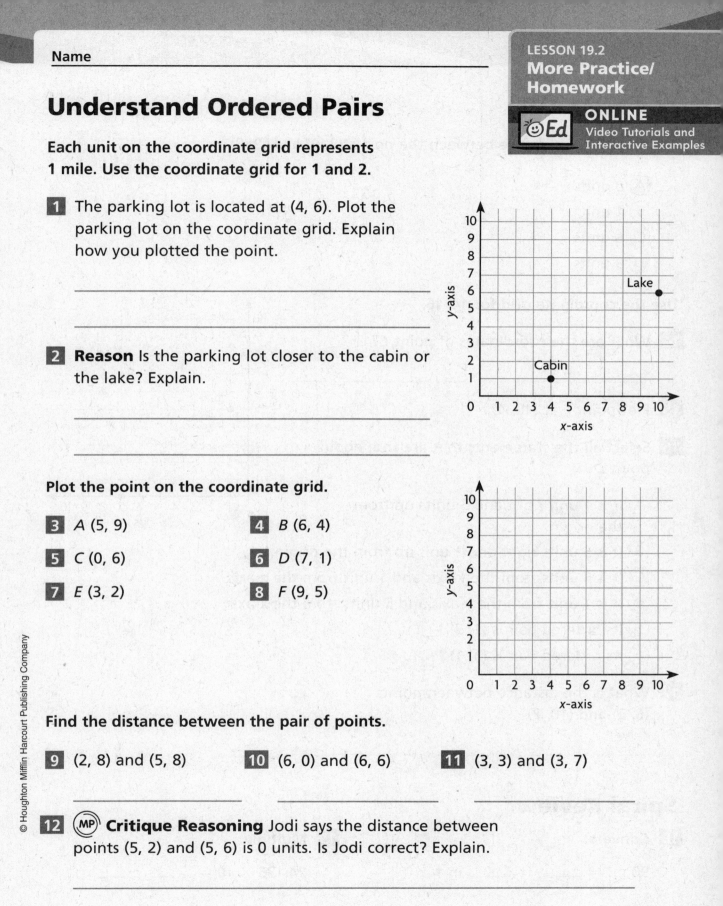

Plot the point on the coordinate grid.

3 *A* (5, 9)   **4** *B* (6, 4)

5 *C* (0, 6)   **6** *D* (7, 1)

7 *E* (3, 2)   **8** *F* (9, 5)

Find the distance between the pair of points.

9 (2, 8) and (5, 8)   **10** (6, 0) and (6, 6)   **11** (3, 3) and (3, 7)

_____   _____   _____

12 (MP) **Critique Reasoning** Jodi says the distance between
points (5, 2) and (5, 6) is 0 units. Is Jodi correct? Explain.

_____

_____

Test Prep

13 What is the distance between the points (8, 0) and (9, 0)?

(A) 0 units

(B) 1 unit

(C) 8 units

(D) 9 units

Use the coordinate grid for 14–16.

14 What are the coordinates of point *C*?

_____

15 Plot point *F* at (10, 4).

16 Select all the statements that are true about point *D*.

(A) It is 1 unit right and 5 units up from the origin.

(B) It is 5 units right and 1 unit up from the origin.

(C) It is 5 units from the *y*-axis and 1 unit from the *x*-axis.

(D) It is 1 unit from the *y*-axis and 5 units from the *x*-axis.

(E) Its ordered pair is (1, 5).

(F) Its ordered pair is (5, 1).

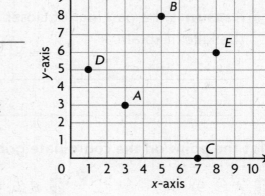

17 What is the distance between points (6, 2) and (10, 2)?

_____

Spiral Review

18 Convert.

90 in. = _____ ft _____ in.

70 oz = _____ lb _____ oz

19 Multiply.

$24.136 \times 10 =$ _____

$174.25 \times \frac{1}{10} =$ _____

LESSON 19.3
**More Practice/
Homework**

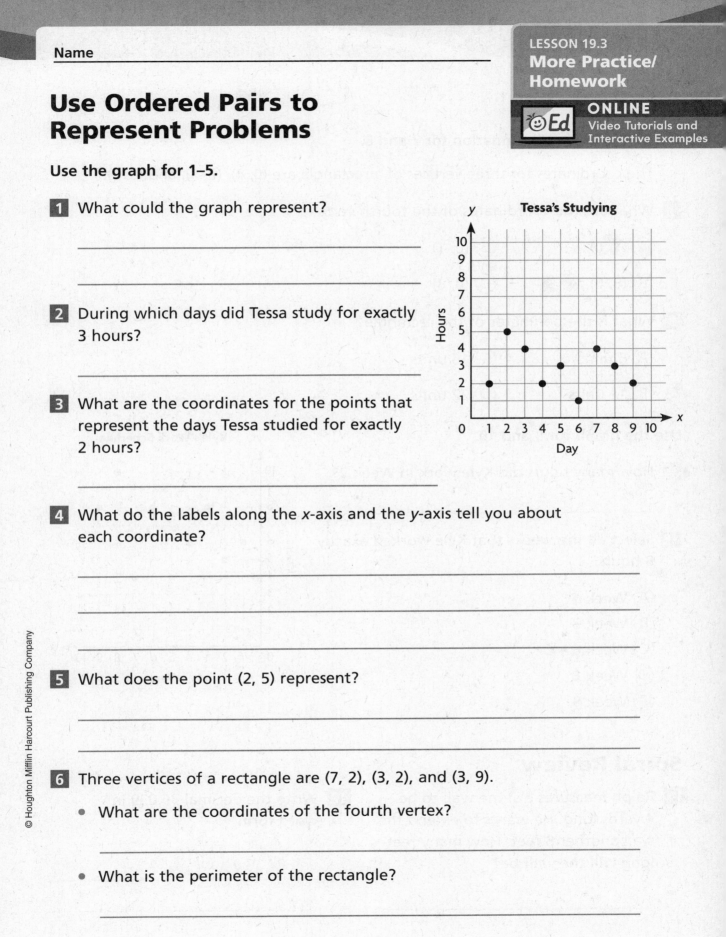
ONLINE
Video Tutorials and
Interactive Examples

Use Ordered Pairs to Represent Problems

Use the graph for 1–5.

1 What could the graph represent?

_____

_____

2 During which days did Tessa study for exactly 3 hours?

_____

3 What are the coordinates for the points that represent the days Tessa studied for exactly 2 hours?

_____

4 What do the labels along the *x*-axis and the *y*-axis tell you about each coordinate?

_____

_____

_____

5 What does the point (2, 5) represent?

_____

_____

6 Three vertices of a rectangle are (7, 2), (3, 2), and (3, 9).

• What are the coordinates of the fourth vertex?

_____

• What is the perimeter of the rectangle?

_____

Test Prep

Use the following information for 7 and 8.

The coordinates for three vertices of a rectangle are (0, 4), (8, 4), and (8, 1).

7 What are the coordinates of the fourth vertex?

Ⓐ (1, 0) Ⓒ (0, 1)

Ⓑ (8, 0) Ⓓ (0, 8)

8 What is the perimeter of the rectangle?

Ⓐ 6 units Ⓒ 16 units

Ⓑ 11 units Ⓓ 22 units

Use the graph for 9 and 10.

9 How many hours did Kyle work in Week 2?

_____

10 Select all the weeks that Kyle worked exactly 8 hours.

Ⓐ Week 1
Ⓑ Week 3
Ⓒ Week 6
Ⓓ Week 8
Ⓔ Week 9

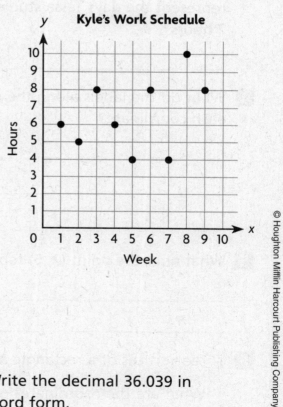

Kyle's Work Schedule

Spiral Review

11 Ralph measures a stone wall to be 4 yards long. He wants to extend the wall another 8 feet. How many feet long will the wall be?

_____

12 Write the decimal 36.039 in word form.

_____

LESSON 19.4
**More Practice/
Homework**

ONLINE
Video Tutorials and
Interactive Examples
😊Ed

Generate and Identify Numerical Patterns

1 (MP) **Use Repeated Reasoning** Li and Amber are writing number patterns. Both patterns start at 2. Li uses the rule "Add 1, then multiply by 3." Amber uses the pattern "Add 2, then multiply by 2." Write the first five ordered pairs with the x-coordinate representing the numbers in Li's pattern and the y-coordinate representing the corresponding numbers in Amber's pattern.

_____

2 (MP) **Reason** Shyla and Diego both run each day. On the first day, Shyla runs for 5 minutes and then follows the rule "Add 4 minutes" each following day. Diego runs for 10 minutes on the first day and then follows the rule "Add 2 minutes" each following day.

- For how many minutes does Shyla
  run each day for her first three days? _____

- For how many minutes does Diego
  run each day for his first three days? _____

- Will there ever by a day where Shyla runs for more minutes
  than Diego? Explain.

_____

_____

_____

_____

3 **Math on the Spot** Rosa plays games at a fair. She can buy 8 game tokens for $1. Each game costs 2 tokens. How many games can she play with 120 tokens? Write a rule and complete the table.

Cost ($)	1	2	3	4	...	15
Tokens	8	16	24	32	...	120
Games	4	8	12	16	...	

Possible rule: _____

Test Prep

4 Cristina writes a number pattern that starts at 9 and follows the rule "Add 7." Which number is in Cristina's pattern?

(A) 16

(C) 25

(B) 21

(D) 34

5 Dev and Rosa are writing number patterns. Dev starts at 4 and uses the rule "Multiply by 3." Rosa starts at 0 and uses the rule "Add 6." What is the first number in Dev's pattern that also appears in Rosa's pattern?

(A) 4

(C) 12

(B) 6

(D) 36

6 Richard writes a number pattern that starts at 1 and follows the rule "Add 1, then multiply by 3." Heather writes a number pattern that starts at 1 and follows the rule "Add 3, then multiply by 2." Write the first five ordered pairs with the *x*-coordinate representing the numbers in Richard's pattern and the *y*-coordinate representing the corresponding numbers in Heather's pattern.

_____

7 Tristan writes a number pattern that starts at 2 and follows the rule "Multiply by 4." Select all the numbers that appear in Tristan's pattern.

(A) 8

(B) 32

(C) 64

(D) 128

(E) 256

Spiral Review

8 Convert.

730 sec = _____ min _____ sec

9 Round 509.373 to the nearest hundredth.

_____

Name _____

Identify and Graph Relationships and Patterns

1 (MP) **Use Tools** Deanna makes lemonade for her friends. The recipe is to add 3 cups of water for every 1 cup of lemonade mix.

- Complete the table. Write the ordered pairs.

Lemonade Mix (in cups)	1		
Water (in cups)			

_____

- Graph the ordered pairs. Label the axes.

- How many cups of water does Deanna need to add if she uses 8 cups of lemonade mix?

_____

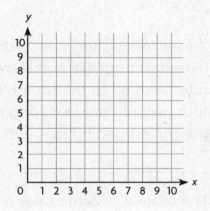

2 (MP) **Critique Reasoning** Elsa says that George's chili is hotter than Lou's chili because the graph shows that the amount of hot sauce in George's chili is always 3 times as much as the amount of hot sauce in Lou's chili. Does Elsa's claim make sense? Explain.

_____

_____

_____

_____

_____

_____

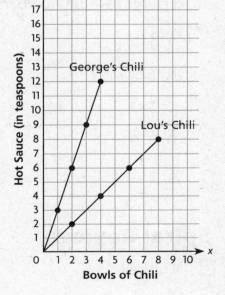

Test Prep

3 The table shows the number of muffins made using different amounts of flour. How many muffins can be made using 5 cups of flour?

Flour (in cups)	1	2	3
Number of muffins	12	24	36

Ⓐ 38

Ⓑ 48

Ⓒ 60

Ⓓ 72

4 Xavier follows the rule "Add 2" to the side length of a square and learns this results in the rule "Add 8" to the square's perimeter. Write four ordered pairs relating the side length and the corresponding perimeter.

_____

5 The table shows the relationship between the number of hours Jamie works and the amount of money he earns. Select all the amounts that Jamie could earn working different whole numbers of hours.

Time Worked (in hours)	0	1	2
Earnings (in dollars)	0	7	14

Ⓐ $15

Ⓑ $21

Ⓒ $42

Ⓓ $50

Ⓔ $63

Spiral Review

6 Multiply.

$$\begin{array}{r} 6.3 \\ \times\ 1.3 \\ \hline \end{array}$$

7 Divide.

728 ÷ 19 _____

Identify and Classify Polygons

1 (MP) **Use Structure** The famous building shown here is shaped like a polygon.

- What type of polygon is this, and how many angles and vertices does it have?

  _____

- How would you know whether the figure is a regular polygon?

  _____

  _____

2 **Open Ended** Draw a polygon. Then explain how you can name the polygon.

_____

_____

(MP) **Use Structure** Name the polygon. Tell whether it is a *regular polygon* or *not a regular polygon*.

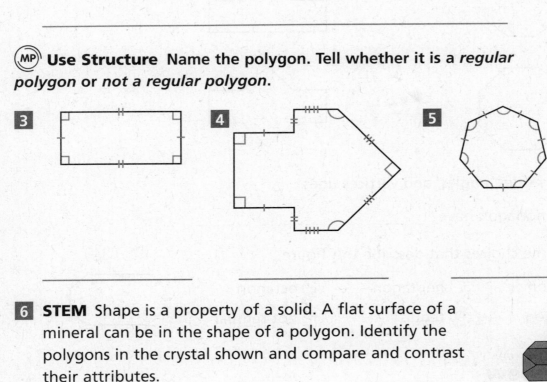

3

4

5

_____   _____   _____

6 **STEM** Shape is a property of a solid. A flat surface of a mineral can be in the shape of a polygon. Identify the polygons in the crystal shown and compare and contrast their attributes.

_____

_____

_____

Test Prep

7 A one-dollar coin from Barbados is shown. Describe why the figure is a polygon, identify the type of polygon, and state whether or not it is a regular polygon.

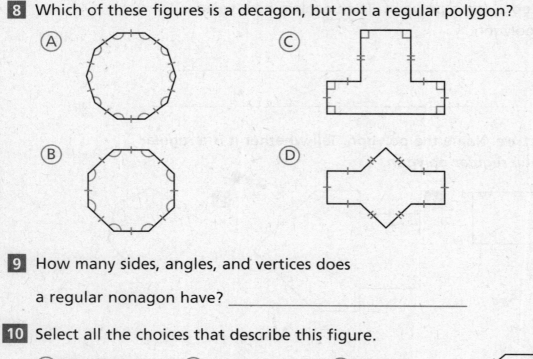

_____

_____

_____

_____

8 Which of these figures is a decagon, but not a regular polygon?

Ⓐ

Ⓒ

Ⓑ

Ⓓ

9 How many sides, angles, and vertices does

a regular nonagon have? _____

10 Select all the choices that describe this figure.

Ⓐ hexagon   Ⓒ heptagon   Ⓔ octagon

Ⓑ nonagon   Ⓓ regular   Ⓕ not regular

Spiral Review

11 Norma buys 4 identical pumpkins for the fall festival and spends $24.60. How much does each pumpkin cost?

_____

12 Divide.

4.8 ÷ 0.3 _____

3.24 ÷ 0.03 _____

Classify and Organize Triangles

1 (MP) **Construct Arguments** A teacher asks students
to draw an equilateral triangle and an isosceles triangle.
Most students draw two different triangles. Lucy draws only
one triangle, and the teacher says it is correct. Describe what
she draws, and explain why it is correct.

_____

_____

2 (MP) **Use Structure** An artist makes triangular-shaped
sculptures using steel rods. The available rods are 12, 13, 14, 15,
or 16 feet long. There are several rods of each length.

- The artist uses a 13-foot and a 15-foot rod for two sides of
  a triangle. Using the available rod lengths for the third side,
  what type(s) of triangles can be made?

  _____

- The artist wants all of the angles in the second triangle to be the same
  measure. What three rod lengths should the artist choose? Explain.

  _____

  _____

(MP) **Use Structure** Classify the triangle. Write *acute*, *obtuse*, or
right. Then write *isosceles*, *scalene*, or *equilateral*.

3

4 45°, 78°, 57°
5 m, 6 m, 7 m

5 4 m 118° 3 m
26° 36°
6 m

_____ _____ _____

6 **Math on the Spot** Shannon said that a triangle with no
congruent sides and one right angle is a scalene obtuse triangle.

Describe her error. _____

_____

Test Prep

7 Select the cell that classifies the triangle by its sides and by its angles.

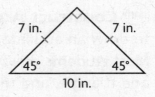

	Scalene	Isosceles	Equilateral
Right	☐	☐	☐
Obtuse	☐	☐	☐
Acute	☐	☐	☐

8 Select all the words that describe the triangle shown.

Ⓐ acute   Ⓒ obtuse   Ⓔ right

Ⓑ scalene   Ⓓ isosceles   Ⓕ equilateral

9 Which shows the possible side lengths and angle measures of an obtuse scalene triangle?

Ⓐ 30°, 60°, 90°
3 in., 4 in., 5 in.

Ⓑ 130°, 25°, 25°
6 in., 6 in., 11 in.

Ⓒ 50°, 60°, 70°
9 in., 10 in., 11 in.

Ⓓ 20°, 40°, 120°
8 in., 15 in., 20 in.

Spiral Review

10 Sofia and Rami write number patterns. Sofia starts with 1 and uses the rule "Multiply by 2, then add 2." Rami starts with 2 and uses the rule "Add 2, then multiply by 2." Write the first five ordered pairs with the *x*-coordinate representing the numbers in Sofia's pattern and the *y*-coordinate representing the corresponding numbers in Rami's pattern. Describe any relationship between the numbers in the two patterns.

_____

_____

11 A rope is 25 feet long. How long is the rope in inches? _____

Classify and Organize Quadrilaterals

1 Art Donna uses a polygon to make a design called a tessellation. Which terms describe the polygon Donna uses to make her design: parallelogram, quadrilateral, rectangle, rhombus, or square?

2 (MP) **Use Structure** Classify the quadrilateral in as many ways as possible. A trapezoid is defined as having at least one pair of parallel sides. Write the letter for the figure.

quadrilateral: _____

parallelogram: _____

rectangle: _____

rhombus: _____

square: _____

trapezoid: _____

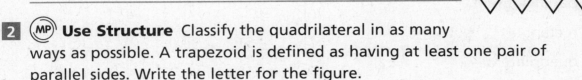

(MP) **Reason** Identify the statement as *true* or *false*.

3 A rectangle is always a parallelogram. _____

4 A rhombus is never a rectangle. _____

5 A parallelogram is always a square. _____

6 Math on the Spot A quadrilateral has exactly 3 congruent sides. Davis claims that the figure must be a rhombus. Why is his claim incorrect? Use diagrams to explain your answer.

_____

_____

Test Prep

7 Select all the words that describe the figure when a trapezoid is defined as having exactly one pair of parallel sides.

Ⓐ square

Ⓑ parallelogram

Ⓒ rectangle

Ⓓ quadrilateral

Ⓔ trapezoid

8 Michelle draws a parallelogram that is not a square. Which statement is true about her parallelogram?

Ⓐ It could be a rectangle, but it could not be a rhombus.

Ⓑ It could be a rhombus, but it could not be a rectangle.

Ⓒ It could be either a rectangle or a rhombus, but not both.

Ⓓ It could be both a rectangle and a rhombus.

Spiral Review

9 Plot points *R*, *S*, and *T* on the coordinate grid.

R(3, 4), *S*(5, 1), *T*(2, 6)

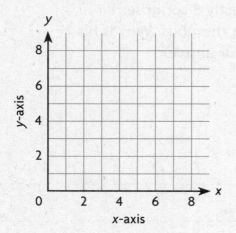

10 Describe how to move from the origin of a coordinate grid to locate the point.

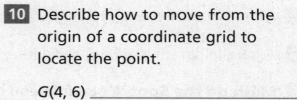

G(4, 6) _____

P(0, 8) _____

Q(2, 1) _____

Name _____

Use Venn Diagrams to Classify Two-Dimensional Figures

ONLINE
Video Tutorials and
Interactive Examples

1 (MP) **Use Structure** National flags from around the world are nearly all non-square rectangles. However, Switzerland has a square flag.

- Draw a Venn diagram to classify and organize triangles, right triangles, quadrilaterals, rectangles, and squares. Shade the regions representing the shapes of the flags described above.

- Does your Venn diagram have one shaded region or more than one shaded region? Explain why.

_____

_____

_____

(MP) **Reason** Write *always, sometimes,* or *never* to complete the statement given the definition of trapezoid represented in this Venn diagram.

2 Rhombuses are _____ parallelograms.

3 Trapezoids are _____ squares.

4 Quadrilaterals are _____ trapezoids.

Quadrilaterals

Parallelograms   Trapezoids

© Houghton Mifflin Harcourt Publishing Company

Test Prep

5 Select all the regions that should be shaded to represent polygons that do not have all congruent sides.

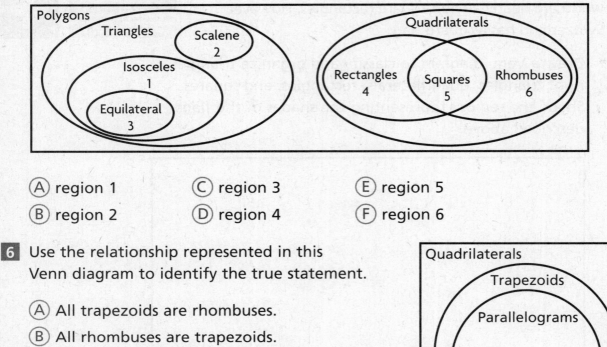

(A) region 1   (C) region 3   (E) region 5

(B) region 2   (D) region 4   (F) region 6

6 Use the relationship represented in this Venn diagram to identify the true statement.

(A) All trapezoids are rhombuses.

(B) All rhombuses are trapezoids.

(C) No trapezoids are rhombuses.

(D) No rhombuses are trapezoids.

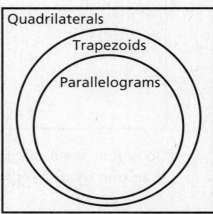

Spiral Review

7 Name the polygon. Tell whether it is a *regular polygon* or *not a regular polygon* and its number of sides.

_____

8 Name a figure that can be placed in each circle of the Venn diagram, and a figure that can be placed in the overlapping area. List the attributes of the figure.

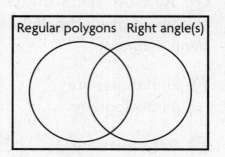

_____

_____

_____

HMH | (into) Math™

My Journal

My Progress on Mathematics Standards

The lessons in your *Into Math* book provide instruction for Mathematics Standards for Grade 5. You can use the following pages to reflect on your learning and record your progress through the standards.

As you learn new concepts, reflect on this learning. Consider inserting a check mark if you understand the concepts or inserting a question mark if you have questions or need help.

	Student Edition Lessons	My Progress
Domain: OPERATIONS AND ALGEBRAIC THINKING		
Cluster: Write and interpret numerical expressions.		
Use parentheses, brackets, or braces in numerical expressions, and evaluate expressions with these symbols.	4.1, 4.3, 4.4	
Write simple expressions that record calculations with numbers, and interpret numerical expressions without evaluating them.	4.1, 4.2	
Cluster: Analyze patterns and relationships.		
Generate two numerical patterns using two given rules. Identify apparent relationships between corresponding terms. Form ordered pairs consisting of corresponding terms from the two patterns, and graph the ordered pairs on a coordinate plane.	19.4, 19.5	

	Student Edition Lessons	My Progress
Domain: NUMBER AND OPERATIONS IN BASE TEN		
Cluster: Understand the place value system.		
Recognize that in a multi-digit number, a digit in one place represents 10 times as much as it represents in the place to its right and $\frac{1}{10}$ of what it represents in the place to its left.	1.1, 13.1	
Explain patterns in the number of zeros of the product when multiplying a number by powers of 10, and explain patterns in the placement of the decimal point when a decimal is multiplied or divided by a power of 10. Use whole-number exponents to denote powers of 10.	1.2, 1.3, 15.1, 17.1	
Read, write, and compare decimals to thousandths.		
• Read and write decimals to thousandths using base-ten numerals, number names, and expanded form, e.g., $347.392 = 3 \times 100 + 4 \times 10 + 7 \times 1 + 3 \times (\frac{1}{10}) + 9 \times (\frac{1}{100}) + 2 \times (\frac{1}{1000})$.	13.2	
• Compare two decimals to thousandths based on meanings of the digits in each place, using $>$, $=$, and $<$ symbols to record the results of comparisons.	13.4	
Use place value understanding to round decimals to any place.	13.3	

Interactive Standards

	Student Edition Lessons	My Progress
Cluster: Perform operations with multi-digit whole numbers and with decimals to hundredths.		
Fluently multiply multi-digit whole numbers using the standard algorithm.	1.4, 1.5, 1.6	
Find whole-number quotients of whole numbers with up to four-digit dividends and two-digit divisors, using strategies based on place value, the properties of operations, and/or the relationship between multiplication and division. Illustrate and explain the calculation by using equations, rectangular arrays, and/or area models.	2.1, 2.2, 2.3, 2.4, 3.1, 3.2, 3.3, 3.4	
Add, subtract, multiply, and divide decimals to hundredths, using concrete models or drawings and strategies based on place value, properties of operations, and/or the relationship between addition and subtraction; relate the strategy to a written method and explain the reasoning used.	14.1, 14.2, 14.3, 14.4, 14.5, 14.6, 15.1, 15.2, 15.3, 15.4, 15.5, 15.6, 16.1, 16.2, 16.3, 17.2, 17.3, 17.4, 17.5, 17.6, 17.7	
Domain: NUMBER AND OPERATIONS–FRACTIONS		
Cluster: Use equivalent fractions as a strategy to add and subtract fractions.		
Add and subtract fractions with unlike denominators (including mixed numbers) by replacing given fractions with equivalent fractions in such a way as to produce an equivalent sum or difference of fractions with like denominators.	6.4, 7.2, 7.3, 7.4, 7.5	

	Student Edition Lessons	My Progress
Solve word problems involving addition and subtraction of fractions referring to the same whole, including cases of unlike denominators, e.g., by using visual fraction models or equations to represent the problem. Use benchmark fractions and number sense of fractions to estimate mentally and assess the reasonableness of answers.	6.1, 6.2, 6.3, 7.1, 7.2, 7.3, 7.6	
Cluster: Apply and extend previous understandings of multiplication and division to multiply and divide fractions.		
Interpret a fraction as division of the numerator by the denominator ($\frac{a}{b} = a \div b$). Solve word problems involving division of whole numbers leading to answers in the form of fractions or mixed numbers, e.g., by using visual fraction models or equations to represent the problem.	3.2, 10.1	
Apply and extend previous understandings of multiplication to multiply a fraction or whole number by a fraction.		
• Interpret the product $(\frac{a}{b}) \times q$ as *a* parts of a partition of *q* into *b* equal parts; equivalently, as the result of a sequence of operations $a \times q \div b$.	8.1, 8.2, 8.3, 8.4, 8.5, 8.7, 9.3	

	Student Edition Lessons	My Progress
• Find the area of a rectangle with fractional side lengths by tiling it with unit squares of the appropriate unit fraction side lengths, and show that the area is the same as would be found by multiplying the side lengths. Multiply fractional side lengths to find areas of rectangles, and represent fraction products as rectangular areas.	8.5, 9.1, 9.4	
Interpret multiplication as scaling (resizing), by:		
• Comparing the size of a product to the size of one factor on the basis of the size of the other factor, without performing the indicated multiplication.	8.6	
• Explaining why multiplying a given number by a fraction greater than 1 results in a product greater than the given number (recognizing multiplication by whole numbers greater than 1 as a familiar case); explaining why multiplying a given number by a fraction less than 1 results in a product smaller than the given number; and relating the principle of fraction equivalence $\frac{a}{b} = \frac{(n \times a)}{(n \times b)}$ to the effect of multiplying $\frac{a}{b}$ by 1.	8.6	

	Student Edition Lessons	My Progress
Solve real world problems involving multiplication of fractions and mixed numbers, e.g., by using visual fraction models or equations to represent the problem.	8.4, 9.1, 9.2, 9.3, 9.4	
Apply and extend previous understandings of division to divide unit fractions by whole numbers and whole numbers by unit fractions.		
• Interpret division of a unit fraction by a non-zero whole number, and compute such quotients.	10.2, 10.3, 11.1, 11.5	
• Interpret division of a whole number by a unit fraction, and compute such quotients.	10.4, 10.5, 11.1, 11.3	
• Solve real world problems involving division of unit fractions by non-zero whole numbers and division of whole numbers by unit fractions, e.g., by using visual fraction models and equations to represent the problem.	10.3, 10.5, 11.2, 11.3, 11.4, 11.5, 11.6	

Domain: MEASUREMENT AND DATA

Cluster: Convert like measurement units within a given measurement system.

Convert among different-sized standard measurement units within a given measurement system (e.g., convert 5 cm to 0.05 m), and use these conversions in solving multi-step, real world problems.	12.1, 12.2, 12.4, 18.1, 18.2, 18.3	

© Houghton Mifflin Harcourt Publishing Company

	Student Edition Lessons	My Progress
Cluster: Represent and interpret data.		
Make a line plot to display a data set of measurements in fractions of a unit ($\frac{1}{2}$, $\frac{1}{4}$, $\frac{1}{8}$). Use operations on fractions for this grade to solve problems involving information presented in line plots.	12.3	
Cluster: Geometric measurement: understand concepts of volume and relate volume to multiplication and to addition.		
Recognize volume as an attribute of solid figures and understand concepts of volume measurement.		
• A cube with side length 1 unit, called a "unit cube," is said to have "one cubic unit" of volume, and can be used to measure volume.	5.1, 5.2	
• A solid figure which can be packed without gaps or overlaps using n unit cubes is said to have a volume of n cubic units.	5.2	
Measure volumes by counting unit cubes, using cubic cm, cubic in, cubic ft, and improvised units.	5.2, 5.3	

	Student Edition Lessons	My Progress
Relate volume to the operations of multiplication and addition and solve real world and mathematical problems involving volume.		
• Find the volume of a right rectangular prism with whole-number side lengths by packing it with unit cubes, and show that the volume is the same as would be found by multiplying the edge lengths, equivalently by multiplying the height by the area of the base. Represent threefold whole-number products as volumes, e.g., to represent the associative property of multiplication.	5.4, 5.5	
• Apply the formulas $V = l \times w \times h$ and $V = b \times h$ for rectangular prisms to find volumes of right rectangular prisms with whole-number edge lengths in the context of solving real world and mathematical problems.	5.4, 5.5	
• Recognize volume as additive. Find volumes of solid figures composed of two non-overlapping right rectangular prisms by adding the volumes of the non-overlapping parts, applying this technique to solve real world problems.	5.6	

Interactive Standards

	Student Edition Lessons	My Progress
Domain: GEOMETRY		
Cluster: Graph points on the coordinate plane to solve real-world and mathematical problems.		
Use a pair of perpendicular number lines, called axes, to define a coordinate system, with the intersection of the lines (the origin) arranged to coincide with the 0 on each line and a given point in the plane located by using an ordered pair of numbers, called its coordinates. Understand that the first number indicates how far to travel from the origin in the direction of one axis, and the second number indicates how far to travel in the direction of the second axis, with the convention that the names of the two axes and the coordinates correspond (e.g., *x*-axis and *x*-coordinate, *y*-axis and *y*-coordinate).	19.1	
Represent real world and mathematical problems by graphing points in the first quadrant of the coordinate plane, and interpret coordinate values of points in the context of the situation.	19.2, 19.3	

© Houghton Mifflin Harcourt Publishing Company

	Student Edition Lessons	My Progress
Cluster: Classify two-dimensional figures into categories based on their properties.		
Understand that attributes belonging to a category of two-dimensional figures also belong to all subcategories of that category.	20.1, 20.2, 20.3, 20.4	
Classify two-dimensional figures in a hierarchy based on properties.	20.1, 20.2, 20.4	

My Learning Summary

As you learn about new concepts, complete a learning summary for each module. A learning summary can include drawings, examples, non-examples, and terminology. It's your learning summary, so show or include information that will help you.

At the end of each module, you will have a summary you can reference to review content for a module test and help you make connections with related math concepts.

My Learning Summary

My Learning Summary

My Learning Summary

My Learning Summary

My Learning Summary

My Learning Summary

My Learning Summary

My Learning Summary

My Learning Summary

My Learning Summary

My Learning Summary

My Learning Summary

My Learning Summary

Name _____

My Learning Summary

My Learning Summary

My Learning Summary

My Learning Summary

My Learning Summary

My Learning Summary

Name _____

My Learning Summary

As you learn about each new term, add notes, drawings, or sentences in the space next to the definition. Doing so will help you remember what each term means.

Pronunciation Key

a add, map	ē equal, tree	m move, seem	o͞o pool, food	u̇ pull, book
ā ace, rate	f fit, half	n nice, tin	p pit, stop	û(r) burn, term
â(r) care, air	g go, log	ng ring, song	r run, poor	yo͞o fuse, few
ä palm, father	h hope, hate	o odd, hot	s see, pass	v vain, eve
b bat, rub	i it, give	ō open, so	sh sure, rush	w win, away
ch check, catch	ī ice, write	ô order, jaw	t talk, sit	y yet, yearn
d dog, rod	j joy, ledge	oi oil, boy	th thin, both	z zest, muse
e end, pet	k cool, take	ou pout, now	<u>th</u> this, bathe	zh vision,
	l look, rule	o͝o took, full	u up, done	pleasure

ə the schwa, an unstressed vowel representing the sound spelled *a* in *above*, *e* in *sicken*, *i* in *possible*, *o* in *melon*, *u* in *circus*

Other symbols:
• separates words into syllables
′ indicates stress on a syllable

My Vocabulary Summary

A

acute angle [ə•kyo͞ot′ ang′gəl] An angle that has a measure less than a right angle (less than 90° and greater than 0°)

ángulo agudo Ángulo que mide menos que un ángulo recto (menos de 90° y más de 0°)

acute triangle [ə•kyo͞ot′ trī′ang•gəl] A triangle that has three acute angles

triángulo acutángulo Triángulo que tiene tres ángulos agudos

Interactive Glossary

angle [ɑngˊgəl] A shape formed by two rays that share the same endpoint

ángulo Figura formada por dos segmentos o semirrectas que tienen un extremo común

area [ârˊē•ə] The measure of the number of unit squares needed to cover a surface

área Medida de la cantidad de cuadrados de una unidad que se necesitan para cubrir una superficie

Associative Property of Addition
[ə•sōˊshē•āt•iv präpˊər•tē əv ə•dishˊən]
The property that states that when the grouping of addends is changed, the sum is the same

propiedad asociativa de la suma Propiedad que establece que cambiar el modo en que se agrupan los sumandos no cambia la suma

Associative Property of Multiplication
[ə•sōˊshē•āt•iv präpˊər•tē əv mul•tə•pli•kāˊshən]
The property that states that factors can be grouped in different ways and still get the same product

propiedad asociativa de la multiplicación Propiedad que establece que cambiar el modo en que se agrupan los factores no cambia el producto

axes [akˊsēzˊ] The two perpendicular lines of a coordinate plane that intersect at the origin

ejes Las dos rectas numéricas perpendiculares del plano de coordenadas que se intersecan en el origen

My Vocabulary Summary

B

base (arithmetic) [bās] A number used as a repeated factor

base (aritmética) Número que se usa como factor repetido

base (geometry) [bās] In two dimensions, one side of a triangle or parallelogram that is used to help find the area; in three dimensions, a plane figure, usually a polygon or circle, by which a three-dimensional figure is measured or named

base (geometría) En dos dimensiones, un lado de un triángulo o paralelogramo que se usa para hallar el área; en tres dimensiones, una figura plana, generalmente un círculo o un polígono, por la que se mide o se nombra una figura tridimensional

benchmark [bench′märk] A familiar number used as a point of reference

punto de referencia Número conocido que se usa como parámetro

C

capacity [kə•pas′i•tē] The amount a container can hold when filled

capacidad Cantidad que puede contener un recipiente cuando se llena

Interactive Glossary

centimeter (cm) [sen′tə•mēt•ər] A metric unit used to measure length or distance; 1 centimeter = 0.01 meter

centímetro (cm) Unidad del sistema métrico que se usa para medir la longitud o la distancia; 1 centímetro = 0.01 metros

common denominator [käm′ən dē•näm′ə•nāt•ər] A common multiple of two or more denominators

denominador común Múltiplo común de dos o más denominadores

common factor [käm′ən fak′tər] A number that is a factor of two or more numbers

factor común Número que es factor de dos o más números

common multiple [käm′ən mul′tə•pəl] A number that is a multiple of two or more numbers

múltiplo común Número que es múltiplo de dos o más números

Commutative Property of Addition [kə•myōōt′ə•tiv präp′ər•tē əv ə•dish′ən] The property that states that when the order of two addends is changed, the sum is the same

propiedad conmutativa de la suma Propiedad que establece que cuando se cambia el orden de dos sumandos, la suma (o total) es la misma

© Houghton Mifflin Harcourt Publishing Company

Commutative Property of Multiplication
[kə•myōōt´ə•tiv präp´ər•tē əv
mul•tə•pli•ka´shən] The property that states
that when the order of two factors is
changed, the product is the same

**propiedad conmutativa de la
multiplicación** Propiedad que establece
que cuando se cambia el orden de dos
factores, el producto es el mismo

compatible numbers [kəm•pat´ə•bəl
num´bərz] Numbers that are easy to
compute with mentally

números compatibles Números con los
que es fácil hacer cálculos mentales

congruent [kən•grōō´ənt] Having the same
size and shape

congruente Que tiene el mismo tamaño
y la misma forma

coordinate grid [kō•ôr´dn•ĭt grĭd] The part
of the coordinate system that describes
all of the ordered pairs on or above the
x-axis and on or to the right of the *y*-axis

cuadrícula de coordenadas La parte
del sistema de coordenadas que describe
todos los pares ordenados en o sobre el
eje *x* y en o a la derecha del eje *y*

coordinate system [kō•ôrd´n•ĭt sis´təm] A
plane formed by the intersection of a
horizontal number line called the *x*-axis
and a vertical number line called the *y*-axis

sistema de coordenadas Plano formado
por la intersección de una recta numérica
horizontal llamada eje *x* y otra vertical
llamada eje *y*

Interactive Glossary

cubic unit [kyo͞oʹbik yo͞oʹnit] A unit used to measure volume such as cubic foot (ft³), cubic meter (m³), and so on

unidad cúbica Unidad que se usa para medir el volumen en pies cúbicos (pie³), metros cúbicos (m³), etc.

---

cup (c) [kup] A customary unit used to measure capacity and liquid volume; 1 cup = 8 fluid ounces

taza (tz) Unidad del sistema usual con la que se mide la capacidad y el volumen de un líquido; 1 taza = 8 onzas fluidas

---

D

decagon [dekʹə•gän] A polygon with ten sides and ten angles

decágono Polígono que tiene diez lados y diez ángulos

---

decimal [desʹə•məl] A number with one or more digits to the right of the decimal point

decimal Número que tiene uno o más dígitos a la derecha del punto decimal

---

decimal point [desʹə•məl point] A symbol used to separate dollars from cents in money, and to separate the ones place from the tenths place in a decimal

punto decimal Símbolo que se usa para separar dólares de centavos y para separar las unidades de los décimos en un número decimal

My Vocabulary Summary

decimeter (dm) [des′i•mēt•ər] A metric unit used to measure length or distance; 10 decimeters = 1 meter

decímetro (dm) Unidad del sistema métrico que se usa para medir la longitud o la distancia; 10 decímetros = 1 metro

denominator [dē•näm′ə•nāt•ər] The number below the bar in a fraction that tells how many equal parts are in the whole or in the group

denominador Número que está debajo de la barra de una fracción y que indica cuántas partes iguales hay en el entero o en el grupo

difference [dif′ər•əns] The answer to a subtraction problem

diferencia Resultado de una resta

dimension [də•men′shən] A measure in one direction

dimensión Medida en una dirección

Distributive Property [di•strib′yoo•tiv präp′ər•tē] The property that states that multiplying a sum by a number is the same as multiplying each addend in the sum by the number and then adding the products

propiedad distributiva Propiedad que establece que multiplicar una suma por un número es lo mismo que multiplicar cada sumando por el número y después sumar los productos

divide [də•vīd′] To separate into equal groups; the inverse operation of multiplication

dividir Separar en grupos iguales; operación inversa de la multiplicación

Interactive Glossary

dividend [div´ə•dend] The number that is to be divided in a division problem

dividendo Número que se divide en una división

division [də•vizh´ən] The process of sharing a number of items to find how many equal groups can be made or how many items will be in each equal group; the inverse operation of multiplication

división Proceso de repartir una cantidad de objetos para hallar cuántos grupos iguales se pueden formar o cuántos objetos habrá en cada grupo; operación inversa de la multiplicación

divisor [də•vī´zər] The number that divides the dividend

divisor Número entre el cual se divide el dividendo

edge [ej] The line segment made where two faces of a solid figure meet

arista Segmento que se forma donde se encuentran dos caras de un cuerpo

elapsed time [ē•lapst´ tīm] The time that passes between the start of an activity and the end of that activity

tiempo transcurrido Tiempo que pasa entre el comienzo de una actividad y el final

equal parts [ē´kwəl pärts] Parts that are exactly the same size

partes iguales Partes que tienen exactamente el mismo tamaño

© Houghton Mifflin Harcourt Publishing Company

My Vocabulary Summary

equation [ē•kwā′zhən] An algebraic or numerical sentence that shows that two quantities are equal

ecuación Enunciado numérico o algebraico que muestra que dos cantidades son iguales

---

equilateral triangle [ē•kwi•lat′ər•əl trī′ang•gəl] A triangle with three congruent sides

triángulo equilátero Triángulo que tiene tres lados congruentes

---

equivalent decimals [ē•kwiv′ə•lənt des′ə•məlz] Decimals that name the same amount

decimales equivalentes Números decimales que indican la misma cantidad

---

equivalent fractions [ē•kwiv′ə•lənt frak′shənz] Fractions that name the same amount or part

fracciones equivalentes Fracciones que nombran la misma cantidad o la misma parte

---

estimate (noun) [es′tə•mit] A number close to an exact amount

estimación Número cercano a una cantidad exacta

---

estimate (verb) [es′tə•māt] To find a number that is close to an exact amount

estimar Hallar un número cercano a una cantidad exacta

Interactive Glossary

evaluate [ē•val′yo͞o•āt] To find the value of a numerical or algebraic expression

evaluar Hallar el valor de una expresión numérica o algebraica

expanded form [ek•span′did fôrm] A way to write numbers by showing the value of each digit

forma desarrollada Manera de escribir los números de forma que muestren el valor de cada uno de los dígitos

exponent [eks′•pōn•ənt] A number that shows how many times the base is used as a factor

exponente Número que muestra cuántas veces se usa la base como factor

F

face [fās] A polygon that is a flat surface of a solid figure

cara Polígono que es una superficie plana de un cuerpo geométrico

fluid ounce (fl oz) [flo͞o′id ouns] A customary unit used to measure liquid capacity and liquid volume;
1 cup = 8 fluid ounces

onza fluida (oz fl) Unidad del sistema usual que se usa para medir la capacidad líquida y el volumen líquido;
1 taza = 8 onzas fluidas

My Vocabulary Summary

foot (ft) [fŏŏt] A customary unit used to measure length or distance;
1 foot = 12 inches

pie Unidad del sistema usual que se usa para medir la longitud o la distancia;
1 pie = 12 pulgadas

formula [fôr′myŏŏ•lə] A set of symbols that expresses a mathematical rule

fórmula Conjunto de símbolos que expresa una regla matemática

fraction [frak′shən] A number that names a part of a whole or a part of a group

fracción Número que nombra una parte de un entero o una parte de un grupo

G

gallon (gal) [gal′ən] A customary unit used to measure capacity and liquid volume;
1 gallon = 4 quarts

galón (gal) Unidad del sistema usual que se usa para medir la capacidad y el volumen líquido;
1 galón = 4 cuartos

gram (g) [gram] A metric unit used to measure mass;
1,000 grams = 1 kilogram

gramo (g) Unidad del sistema métrico que se usa para medir la masa;
1,000 gramos = 1 kilogramo

Interactive Glossary

greater than (>) [grāt′ər <u>th</u>an] A symbol used to compare two numbers or two quantities when the greater number or greater quantity is given first

mayor que (>) Símbolo que se usa para comparar dos números o dos cantidades cuando el número o la cantidad mayor se da primero

H

height [hīt] The length of a perpendicular from the base to the top of a two-dimensional or three-dimensional figure

altura Longitud de una línea perpendicular desde la base hasta la parte superior de una figura bidimensional o tridimensional

heptagon [hep′tə•gän] A polygon with seven sides and seven angles

heptágono Polígono que tiene siete lados y siete ángulos

hexagon [hek′sə•gän] A polygon with six sides and six angles

hexágono Polígono que tiene seis lados y seis ángulos

hundredth [hun′drədth] One of 100 equal parts

centésimo Una de 100 partes iguales

My Vocabulary Summary

I

inch (in.) [inch] A customary unit used to measure length or distance; 12 inches = 1 foot

pulgada (pulg) Unidad del sistema usual que se usa para medir la longitud o la distancia; 12 pulgadas = 1 pie

inverse operations [in′vûrs äp•ə•rā′shənz] Opposite operations, or operations that undo each other, such as addition and subtraction or multiplication and division

operaciones inversas Operaciones opuestas u operaciones que se cancelan entre sí, como la suma y la resta o la multiplicación y la división

isosceles triangle [ī•säs′ə•lēz trī′ang•gəl] A triangle with at least two congruent sides

triángulo isósceles Triángulo con dos lados congruentes

K

kilogram (kg) [kil′ō•gram] A metric unit used to measure mass; 1 kilogram = 1,000 grams

kilogramo (kg) Unidad del sistema métrico que se usa para medir la masa; 1 kilogramo = 1,000 gramos

Interactive Glossary

kilometer (km) [kə•läm′ət•ər] A metric unit used to measure length or distance; 1 kilometer = 1,000 meters

kilómetro Unidad del sistema métrico que se usa para medir la longitud o la distancia; 1 kilómetro = 1,000 metros

L

less than (<) [less than] A symbol used to compare two numbers or two quantities, with the lesser number or lesser quantity given first

menor que (<) Símbolo que se usa para comparar dos números o dos cantidades cuando el número menor o la cantidad menor se da primero

line plot [līn plät] A graph that shows frequency of data along a number line

diagrama de puntos Gráfica que muestra la frecuencia de los datos en una recta numérica

liquid volume [lik′wid väl′yoom] The measure of the space a liquid occupies

volumen de un líquido La medida del espacio que ocupa un líquido

liter (L) [lēt′ər] A metric unit used to measure capacity and liquid volume; 1 liter = 1,000 milliliters

litro (L) Unidad del sistema métrico que se usa para medir la capacidad y el volumen líquido; 1 litro = 1,000 mililitros

My Vocabulary Summary

meter (m) [mĕt′ər] A metric unit used to measure length or distance; 1 meter = 100 centimeters

metro (m) Unidad del sistema métrico que se usa para medir la longitud o la distancia; 1 metro = 100 centímetros

mile (mi) [mīl] A customary unit used to measure length or distance; 1 mile = 5,280 feet

milla (mi) Unidad del sistema usual que se usa para medir la longitud o la distancia; 1 milla = 5,280 pies

milligram (mg) [mil′i•gram] A metric unit used to measure mass; 1,000 milligrams = 1 gram

miligramo Unidad del sistema métrico que se usa para medir la masa; 1,000 miligramos = 1 gramo

milliliter (mL) [mil′i•lēt•ər] A metric unit used to measure capacity and liquid volume; 1,000 milliliters = 1 liter

mililitro (mL) Unidad del sistema métrico que se usa para medir la capacidad y el volumen líquido; 1,000 mililitros = 1 litro

millimeter (mm) [mil′i•mēt•ər] A metric unit used to measure length or distance; 1,000 millimeters = 1 meter

milímetro (mm) Unidad del sistema métrico que se usa para medir la longitud o la distancia; 1,000 milímetros = 1 metro

Interactive Glossary

My Vocabulary Summary

mixed number [mikst num′bər] A number that is made up of a whole number and a fraction

número mixto Número formado por un número entero y una fracción

multiple [mul′tə•pəl] The product of two counting numbers is a multiple of each of those numbers

múltiplo El producto de dos números naturales es un múltiplo de cada uno de esos números

multiplication [mul•tə•pli•kā′shən] A process to find the total number of items made up of equal-sized groups, or to find the total number of items in a given number of groups; it is the inverse operation of division.

multiplicación Proceso de hallar la cantidad total de objetos formados en grupos del mismo tamaño o la cantidad total de objetos que hay en una determinada cantidad de grupos; operación inversa de la división

multiply [mul′tə•plī] When you combine equal groups, you can multiply to find how many in all; the inverse operation of division

multiplicar Combinar grupos iguales para hallar cuántos hay en total; operación inversa de la división

My Vocabulary Summary

nonagon [nän′ə•gän] A polygon with nine sides and nine angles

eneágono Polígono que tiene nueve lados y nueve ángulos

number line [num′bər līn] A line on which numbers can be located

recta numérica Recta donde se pueden ubicar números

numerator [noo′mər•āt•ər] The number above the bar in a fraction that tells how many equal parts of the whole or group are being considered

numerador Número que está arriba de la barra en una fracción y que indica cuántas partes iguales de un entero o de un grupo se consideran

numerical expression [noo•mer′i•kəl ek•spresh′ən] A mathematical phrase that uses only numbers and operation signs

expresión numérica Frase matemática en la que solamente se usan números y signos de operaciones

O

obtuse angle [äb•toos′ ang′gəl] An angle whose measure is greater than 90° and less than 180°

ángulo obtuso Ángulo que mide más de 90° y menos de 180°

My Vocabulary Summary

obtuse triangle [äb•toos′ trī′ang•gəl] A triangle that has one obtuse angle

triángulo obtusángulo Triángulo que tiene un ángulo obtuso

octagon [äk′tə•gän] A polygon with eight sides and eight angles

octágono Polígono que tiene ocho lados y ocho ángulos

ordered pair [ôr′dərd pâr] A pair of numbers used to locate a point on a grid; the first number tells the left-right position and the second number tells the up-down position.

par ordenado Par de números que se usan para ubicar un punto en una cuadrícula; el primer número indica la posición izquierda-derecha y el segundo número indica la posición arriba-abajo.

order of operations [ôr′dər əv äp•ə•rā′shənz] A special set of rules which gives the order in which calculations are done in an expression

orden de las operaciones Conjunto especial de reglas que indican el orden en el que se deben realizar las operaciones en una expresión

origin [ôr′ə•jin] The point where the two axes of a coordinate grid intersect; (0, 0)

origen Punto donde se intersecan los dos ejes de un plano de coordenadas; (0, 0)

My Vocabulary Summary

ounce (oz) [ouns] A customary unit used to measure weight; 16 ounces = 1 pound

onza (oz) Unidad del sistema usual que se usa para medir el peso; 16 onzas = 1 libra

parallel lines [pâr´ə•lel līnz] Lines in the same plane that never intersect and are always the same distance apart

líneas paralelas Líneas que están en el mismo plano, que no se cortan nunca y que siempre están separadas por la misma distancia

parallelogram [pâr•ə•lel´ə•gram] A quadrilateral whose opposite sides are parallel and have the same length, or are congruent

paralelogramo Cuadrilátero cuyos lados opuestos son paralelos y tienen la misma longitud, es decir, son congruentes

parentheses [pə•ren´thə•sēz] The symbols used to show which operation or operations in an expression should be done first

paréntesis Símbolos que se usan para mostrar cuál de las operaciones de una expresión se debe hacer primero

Interactive Glossary

partial product [pärˈshəl prädˈəkt] A method of multiplying in which the ones, tens, hundreds, and so on are multiplied separately and then the products are added together

producto parcial Método de multiplicación en el que se multiplican por separado las unidades, las decenas, las centenas, etc. y después se suman los productos

partial quotient [pärˈshəl kwōˈshəntz] A method of dividing in which multiples of the divisor are subtracted from the dividend and then the quotients are added together

cociente parcial Método de división en el que los múltiplos del divisor se restan del dividendo y después se suman los cocientes

pattern [patˈərn] An ordered set of numbers or objects; the order helps you predict what will come next

patrón Conjunto ordenado de números u objetos en el que el orden ayuda a predecir el siguiente número u objeto

pentagon [penˈtə•gän] A polygon with five sides and five angles

pentágono Polígono que tiene cinco lados y cinco ángulos

perpendicular lines [pər•pən•dikˈyo͞o•lər līnz] Two lines that intersect to form four right angles

líneas perpendiculares Dos líneas que se intersecan y forman cuatro ángulos rectos

My Vocabulary Summary

pint (pt) [pīnt] A customary unit used to measure capacity and liquid volume; 1 pint = 2 cups

pinta (pt) Unidad del sistema usual que se usa para medir la capacidad y el volumen líquido; 1 pinta = 2 tazas

place value [plās val'yo͞o] The value of each digit in a number based on the location of the digit

valor posicional Valor de cada uno de los dígitos de un número, según el lugar que ocupa el dígito

polygon [päl'i•gän] A closed plane figure formed by three or more line segments

polígono Figura plana y cerrada formada por tres o más segmentos

pound (lb) [pound] A customary unit used to measure weight; 1 pound = 16 ounces

libra (lb) Unidad del sistema usual que se usa para medir el peso; 1 libra = 16 onzas

power [pou'ər] A number produced by raising a base to an exponent

potencia Número que resulta al elevar una base a un exponente

product [präd'əkt] The answer to a multiplication problem

producto Resultado de una multiplicación

Interactive Glossary

Q

quadrilateral [kwä•dri•lat´ər•əl] A polygon with four sides and four angles

cuadrilátero Polígono que tiene cuatro lados y cuatro ángulos

quart (qt) [kwôrt] A customary unit used to measure capacity and liquid volume; 1 quart = 2 pints

cuarto (qt) Unidad del sistema usual que se usa para medir la capacidad y el volumen líquido; 1 cuarto = 2 pintas

quotient [kwō´shənt] The number that results from dividing

cociente Número que resulta de una división

R

rectangle [rek´tang•gel] A parallelogram with four right angles

rectángulo Paralelogramo que tiene cuatro ángulos rectos

regroup [rē•groop´] To exchange amounts of equal value to rename a number

reagrupar Intercambiar cantidades de valores equivalentes para volver a escribir un número

My Vocabulary Summary

regular polygon [reg′yə•lar päl′i•gän] A polygon in which all sides are congruent and all angles are congruent

polígono regular Polígono cuyos lados y ángulos son todos congruentes

remainder [ri•mān′dər] The amount left over when a number cannot be divided equally

residuo Cantidad que sobra cuando un número no se puede dividir en partes iguales

rhombus [räm′bəs] A parallelogram with four equal, or congruent, sides

rombo Paralelogramo que tiene cuatro lados congruentes o iguales

right angle [rīt ang′gəl] An angle that forms a square corner and has a measure of 90°

ángulo recto Ángulo que forma una esquina cuadrada y mide 90°

right rectangular prism [rīt rek•tang′gyə•lər priz′əm] A three-dimensional figure in which all six faces are rectangles

prisma recto rectangular Figura tridimensional con las seis caras rectangulares

right triangle [rīt trī′ang•gəl] A triangle that has a right angle

triángulo rectángulo Triángulo que tiene un ángulo recto

Interactive Glossary

round [round] To replace a number with one that is simpler and is approximately the same size as the original number

redondear Reemplazar un número por otro más simple que tenga aproximadamente el mismo tamaño que el número original

S

scalene triangle [skā′lēn trī′ang•gəl] A triangle with no congruent sides

triángulo escaleno Triángulo cuyos lados no son congruentes

sequence [sē′kwəns] An ordered list of numbers

secuencia Lista ordenada de números

square [skwâr] A polygon with four equal, or congruent, sides and four right angles

cuadrado Polígono que tiene cuatro lados congruentes y cuatro ángulos rectos

sum [sum] The answer to an addition problem

suma o total Resultado de una suma

T

tenth [tenth] One of ten equal parts

décimo Una de diez partes iguales

term [tûrm] A number in a sequence

término Número de una secuencia

---

thousandth [thou′zəndth] One of one thousand equal parts

milésimo Una de 1,000 partes iguales

---

ton (T) [tun] A customary unit used to measure weight; 1 ton = 2,000 pounds

tonelada (t) Unidad del sistema usual que se usa para medir el peso; 2,000 libras = 1 tonelada

---

trapezoid [trap′i•zoid] *exclusive* A quadrilateral with exactly one pair of parallel sides

trapecio *exclusivo* Cuadrilátero con exactamente un par de lados paralelos.

---

trapezoid [trap′i•zoid] *inclusive* A quadrilateral with at least one pair of parallel sides

trapecio *inclusivo* Cuadrilátero con un par de lados paralelos.

---

triangle [trī′ang•gəl] A polygon with three sides and three angles

triángulo Polígono que tiene tres lados y tres ángulos

U

unit cube [yōō′nit kyōōb] A cube that has a length, width, and height of 1 unit

cubo unitario Cubo cuya longitud, ancho y altura es de 1 unidad

Interactive Glossary

unit fraction [yoo´nit frak´shən] A fraction that has 1 as a numerator

fracción unitaria Fracción que tiene un número 1 como numerador

Venn diagram [ven dī´ə•gram] A diagram that shows relationships among sets of things

diagrama de Venn Diagrama que muestra las relaciones entre conjuntos de cosas

vertex [vûr´teks] The point where two or more rays meet; the point of intersection of two sides of a polygon; the point of intersection of three (or more) edges of a solid figure; the top point of a cone; the plural of vertex is vertices.

vértice Punto en el que se encuentran dos o más semirrectas; punto de intersección de dos lados de un polígono; punto de intersección de tres (o más) aristas de un cuerpo geométrico; punto superior de un cono

volume [väl´yoom] The measure of the space a solid figure occupies

volumen Medida del espacio que ocupa un cuerpo geométrico

W

weight [wāt] How heavy an object is

peso Cuán pesado es un objeto

whole [hōl] All of the parts of a figure or group

entero Todas las partes de una figura o de un grupo

X

***x*-axis** [eks ak′sis] The horizontal number line on a coordinate plane

eje de la *x* Recta numérica horizontal de un plano de coordenadas

***x*-coordinate** [eks kō•ôrd′n•it] The first number in an ordered pair; tells the distance to move right or left from (0, 0)

coordenada *x* Primer número de un par ordenado que indica la distancia desde la cual hay que moverse hacia la derecha o la izquierda desde (0, 0)

Interactive Glossary

yard (yd) [yärd] A customary unit used to measure length or distance; 1 yard = 3 feet

yarda (yd) Unidad del sistema usual que se usa para medir la longitud o la distancia; 1 yarda = 3 pies

***y*-axis** [wī ak′sis] The vertical number line on a coordinate plane

eje de la *y* Recta numérica vertical de un plano de coordenadas

***y*-coordinate** [wī kō•ôrd′n•it] The second number in an ordered pair; tells the distance to move up or down from (0, 0)

coordenada *y* Segundo número de un par ordenado que indica la distancia desde la cual hay que moverse hacia arriba o hacia abajo desde (0, 0)

LENGTH

Metric

1 meter (m) = 1,000 millimeters (mm)

1 meter = 100 centimeters (cm)

1 meter = 10 decimeters (dm)

1 dekameter (dam) = 10 meters

1 hectometer (hm) = 100 meters

1 kilometer (km) = 1,000 meters

Customary

1 foot (ft) = 12 inches (in.)

1 yard (yd) = 3 feet

1 yard = 36 inches

1 mile (mi) = 1,760 yards

1 mile = 5,280 feet

CAPACITY AND LIQUID VOLUME

Metric

1 liter (L) = 1,000 milliliters (mL)

1 liter = 100 centiliters (cL)

1 liter = 10 deciliters (dL)

1 dekaliter (daL) = 10 liters

1 hectoliter (hL) = 100 liters

1 kiloliter (kL) = 1,000 liters

Customary

1 cup (c) = 8 fluid ounces (fl oz)

1 pint (pt) = 2 cups

1 quart (qt) = 2 pints

1 quart = 4 cups

1 gallon (gal) = 4 quarts

MASS/WEIGHT

1 gram (g) = 1,000 milligrams (mg)

1 gram = 100 centigrams (cg)

1 gram = 10 decigrams (dg)

1 pound (lb) = 16 ounces (oz)

1 ton (T) = 2,000 pounds

Table of Measures

TIME

1 minute (min) = 60 seconds (sec)

1 half hour = 30 minutes

1 hour (hr) = 60 minutes

1 day = 24 hours

1 week (wk) = 7 days

1 year (yr) = about 52 weeks

1 year = 12 months (mo)

1 year = 365 days

1 leap year = 366 days

1 decade = 10 years

1 century = 100 years

1 millennium = 1,000 years

SYMBOLS

$=$	is equal to	$\overleftrightarrow{AB}$	line AB
$\neq$	is not equal to	$\overline{AB}$	line segment AB
$>$	is greater than	$\overrightarrow{AB}$	ray AB
$<$	is less than	$\angle ABC$	angle ABC, or angle B
$(2, 3)$	ordered pair (x, y)	$\triangle ABC$	triangle ABC
$\perp$	is perpendicular to	$°$	degree
$\parallel$	is parallel to	$°C$	degrees Celsius
		$°F$	degrees Fahrenheit

FORMULAS

Perimeter

Polygon $\quad$ P = sum of the lengths of sides

Rectangle $\quad$ $P = (2 \times l) + (2 \times w)$

Square $\quad$ $P = 4 \times s$

Area

Rectangle $\quad$ $A = l \times w$
$A = b \times h$

Volume

Rectangular Prism $\quad$ $V = l \times w \times h$, or
$V = B \times h$

B = area of base shape,
h = height of prism